Max Schlemmer, Hawaii's King of Laysan Island

To the Rashids - Jeff and Susie
This story is a peek
into the other side of "Paradise."
Aloha
Tom E Unger
Kailua Kona Hawaii 1-2-10

Max Schlemmer, Hawaii's King of Laysan Island

Tom E. Unger

iUniverse, Inc.
New York Lincoln Shanghai

Max Schlemmer, Hawaii's King of Laysan Island

iUniverse, Inc.

For information address:
iUniverse, Inc.
2021 Pine Lake Road, Suite 100
Lincoln, NE 68512
www.iuniverse.com

ISBN: 0-595-29988-1 (pbk)
ISBN: 0-595-66103-3 (cloth)

Printed in the United States of America

This book is dedicated to my late Aunt Tess, Therese Julia Schlemmer Bredehoft. It was her idea and wish to write the story of Max Schlemmer, her beloved father.

"The evil that men do lives after them. The good is oft interred with their bones."

—Shakespeare, Julius Caesar, Act III, Scene II

Contents

ACKNOWLEDGMENTS

My sincere thanks to my late Aunt Tess, Therese Schlemmer Bredehoft, who wanted to tell the story of her father. To my Aunt Helene Schlemmer Brown for her advice and rare photographs. To my late Uncle Eric Laysan Schlemmer and family for rare unpublished documents. To my calabash cousin Shirley Bomke Craddock for the genealogy of my mother's ancestors. To granddaughter Laysan Cartwright Unger for a great typing job. To Maryanne Raphael for pushing this project to fruition. To Donald Johnson for his computer expertise. To my dear wife Janice who helped put the story together and kept my feet to the fire.

INTRODUCTION

This is the story of my grandfather, Maximillian Joseph August Schlemmer who dreamed of establishing a "Kingdom" on the island of Laysan.

Laysan is a tiny island about 1½ miles by 1 mile wide, about 800 miles northwest of Honolulu. The island is located in the center of the Northwest Hawaiian Islands which extend about 1200 miles into the northwest Pacific.

Max's life was intimately involved with the island of Laysan from 1893 through 1915. Max established his home there in the early years. Five of his children were born there including my Mother, Ottilie Laysan Schlemmer Unger in 1897.

This is also the story of the life and death of an island.

1

MAX'S EARLY LIFE

My grandfather, Maximilian Joseph Schlemmer, was born in Scheibenhardt, April 13, 1856, to German parents in the French province of Alsace Lorraine. From his earliest days it was apparent that this gangly auburn haired kid could not get along with his family. There were many disputes as to how he should go about preparing for his future. Attending school was not a priority for young Max. What was a priority was how he could find his way to America. He was prepared to handle whatever lay ahead.

In the year of 1871, as the Prussian army stormed across the French border to claim the province of Alsace Lorraine for the greater glory of the German Empire, fifteen-year old Max Schlemmer boarded a sailing vessel bound for New York.

New York was a shock to Max, the young immigrant. He had never experienced the impact on his senses from such an overwhelming mass of humanity. Not just the sights, sounds and smells but the babble of strange tongues confronted him wherever he went. He at last found German-speaking people from whom he rented a room in a German boarding house. He then proceeded to tramp the streets looking for work.

Max soon realized that America was the land of golden opportunity for those people with a skill who could also converse in the English language. His assets included neither. As the days slipped by and his money began to run out and as panic began to grip his soul, Max was able to get a job in a butcher shop as a delivery boy.

Being a delivery boy for a German butcher was not what Max had in mind when he escaped from the old country. Each night he dragged himself back to his room and poured over the want ads in the New York German newspaper, *Staat Zeitung*.

After several weeks of searching he was rewarded. Rather than a want ad, it was a small article that caught his attention. The article stated that if a young man wanted to see the world on sailing ships he was to contact John O. Spicer. The address was near the port city of New London, Connecticut.

John Spicer was the skipper of the bark *Nile*. He welcomed the young immigrant with warmth and geniality and invited him aboard his ship. Shortly thereafter they set sail for whaling grounds along Greenland's Icy Mountain. When they returned, Max discovered exactly what Captain Spicer had in mind for him. Captain Spicer offered Max a job on his farm. In exchange for Max's labor, the captain would teach him English and navigation. This did not sit well with Max. He refused the offer.

Once again the rebel Max was on the road. This time he headed to New Bedford, Massachusetts. From there, he was launched on a whaling career that lasted fourteen years.

The hunting and slaughtering of whales was a dirty and dangerous business. Making matters worse was the fact that by the time Max signed aboard his first whaling ship, whale herds in the Atlantic were depleted as were those in the warm waters of the Pacific. As a result of this mass slaughter, the hunt for the whale was focused on the frigid North Pacific.

There were few men like Max, who were willing to expose themselves to such harsh elements. So it was not unusual for Max to wake up aboard ship in the morning on the high seas to find a new member of the crew in the bunk below him. The poor fellow had been "shanghaied." "Shanghaiing" was a crude but sometimes effective means for recruiting seamen. They were slugged or drugged and brought aboard ship at night. Once on the high seas they had little choice other than to sign aboard as members of the crew.

One day in the early 1930's while "talking story" with grandfather Max on the large, spacious veranda of his "plantation green" house on Wilder avenue, in Honolulu, I was enchanted as he told me about the hazards of whaling in the far northwest Pacific. He said there were times without warning that white foam would burst over the bow of the ship. You were chilled to the marrow of your bones. Riggings froze and men froze with them. Giant waves rolled over the ship washing men overboard. Max himself had been lashed to the wheel housing of the ship while steering through many a raging storm. Howling wind would rake the ship, shredding sails while splintering the ship's masts.

But there were hazards beyond the natural disasters aboard a whaling ship. Max went on to say that after he had been at sea for several years he became a crewman on a whaleboat. There, danger was vastly increased. His task was to steer the boat at the direction of the harpooner, who stood at the bow of the boat while the four-man crew rowed toward the whale.

There were times when a harpooned whale would dive (with a loud swish), taking the boat and crew to the bottom. At other times a whale in its agony might thrash about with its massive tail (fluke) and shatter the fragile boat leaving its crew abandoned in icy water. Max considered himself lucky. He was often taken on a wild ride by the harpooned whale over the waves, known as a Nantucket Sleigh ride. It ended when the whale died.

I was twelve years old when Grandpa Max passed away. Over the years I have heard many tales and half-truths about him. I believe I have uncovered his real life. So my story continues.

Max first saw Hawaii in 1876, when the ship he was on, the *Cleone,* made its way from San Juan Fernandez Islands off the coast of Chili, bound for Honolulu. It had been a long and arduous voyage.

James Stanton, the ship's captain, became ill and the ship's first officer now in charge, altered course because of a serious shortage of water and rations and docked at Hilo Bay on the Big Island of Hawaii. My Aunt Tess always told about how proud Max was to say that he had visited Robinson Crusoe's island on his way to Honolulu, on the island of Oahu.

Once in Honolulu, Captain Nye took over the helm of the *Cleone* and sailed into the sea of Okhotsk, Russian territorial waters, where he decided to do a little cod fishing. It wasn't long before a Russian man-of-war arrived to interrupt his plans.

The *Cleone* was able to escape the Russian ship but as it sailed into the Arctic Ocean by way of the Bearing Sea it ran into a powerful storm. The *Cleone* was disabled and had to be abandoned. Fortunately the *Progress* was close by and Captain Nye and his crew were transferred aboard and taken to San Francisco.

In the early 1880's Max signed aboard the *Mount Walruston* out of San Francisco. Also aboard ship was another seaman with whom Max soon became a close friend. Klaus was a young swashbuckling Prussian who had apparently been exiled to the sea for reasons known only to him and his parents.

Besides both being German, Max and Klaus had another thing in common; they both hated the *Mount Walruston's* First Officer. He was drunk and surly most of the time. When he strode on deck there were crew members that would shudder with fear as he approached them.

If a seaman were ever to address the First Officer without removing his hat the poor fellow would be knocked down from a blow struck by this powerful and vicious First Officer. The same was true if a seaman failed to remove the pipe from his mouth when he addressed the First Officer.

Klaus, whose face bore a few scars from fencing duels, was a person whom the First Officer had somehow overlooked. This could have been a fatal mistake on his part. For the wily Prussian Klaus had set the time and place at which the assassination of the First Officer was to happen. After a long and serious discussion that lasted late into the night, Max convinced Klaus that his plan was too radical. They agreed that it would be best if they both quietly disappeared some night. And so they did just that.

On a quiet moonless night while the *Mount Walruston* lay anchored at Tres Marias Islands off the coast of Mexico, Max tells us that he, Klaus and two others, went over the side of the ship and boarded a small whale boat loaded with valuable whaling gear. Stealthily they rowed away and disappeared into the night. By early morning they had stashed the boat, well camouflaged in a cove, set up camp, and waited.

Several days later, the *Mount Walruston* set sail and the self-imposed castaways were free. Tres Marias was a port of call and two of their crew members were able to sign aboard ships and sail away.

Max and Klaus were willing to wait and barter for their passage to the Sandwich Islands (Hawaii). By the end of the week, they learned that the *Newton Booth* was preparing to sail to Hawaii. So the two castaways went aboard the ship and offered Captain Carrel a whaleboat and a large quantity of whaling tools and equipment in exchange for their passage. The *Newton Booth* was low on supplies and the Captain was reluctant to take on additional crew members. Nevertheless, after giving it some thought, Captain Carrel apparently realized that he could replenish his larder with the money he would receive from the sale of the boat and equipment. With this in mind, he agreed to take Max and Klaus aboard. The Captain had then become part of the conspiracy.

As Max explained the following episode to my Aunt Tess, he maintained that it was the cleverest and one of the most daring feats he had ever witnessed at sea.

The weather was bad and the ocean was rough as the *Newton Booth*, directed by Max and Klaus, made its way along the coast to where the booty lay hidden. With due concern for an encounter with a submerged reef, Captain Carrel dropped anchor somewhat further from shore than Klaus had anticipated. Klaus now feared that the small whale boat in such high surf and rough water would either swamp or capsize when loaded with so much loose and heavy cargo. He devised a plan that would allow the cargo to be hauled aboard the *Newton Booth* separately from the boat.

With little concern for his safety, Klaus climbed under the ships rail and with a light rope tied about his waist, plunged into the angry sea. With powerful strokes he made his way through waves that at times hid him from view.

Once on shore he hauled in from the ship the light rope that had been about his waist. On the end of the rope was a heavier rope to which he tied at various intervals, the many lances, harpoons, oars, and masts. Max and the crew on the *Newton Booth* quickly hauled these aboard. Klaus then seated himself on a bundle of sails and rowed back through the pounding surf to the waiting ship and a hero's welcome.

When the *Newton Booth* docked at Honolulu, Captain Carrel became concerned that the *Mount Walruston* might also dock at Honolulu. He suggested that both Max and Klaus falsify their names on the ship's manifest.

Klaus took no chances. He hurriedly shipped out on the *Martha Davis* bound for San Francisco. Max wanted to remain in Hawaii. But it was not long before word got out in Honolulu about what happened at Tres Marias.

Max realized it was just a matter of time before he would be apprehended. He could change his name on the ship's manifest but he had to admit that he could not change his appearance. There was no doubt. He was that tall "haole" with auburn hair. In a crowd of local citizens, he stuck out like a carrot in a taro patch. It was time to leave Hawaii but by then he knew that Hawaii would be his home some day.

Max, now a fugitive from justice, took passage on the *Edward James* bound for Tahiti and the South Seas. With regard to his trip aboard the *Edward James*, Max recalls that the owner, who was aboard when the ship sailed from Honolulu, died when the ship was three days out.

The ship's captain had little control over the crew. He was usually drunk and the crew spent most of their time brawling and fighting. Max was unscathed and thankful to depart the ship once it reached Tahiti. Max decided to stay in Tahiti until things cooled down in Hawaii. Other than the fact that he had a miserable trip to Tahiti, as he told the story, nothing is known about Max until he returned to Hawaii.

Max returned to Hawaii from the South Seas in 1885. He went directly to the island of Kauai. He had heard about the German settlement there. Lihue was known as "German Town." H. Hackfeld, a German company, owned and operated the largest sugar plantation here.

Most of their workers were recruited from Germany. Before leaving Germany, the workers signed a contract stipulating their wages and benefits. Workers were to be paid $16.00 a month for the first year and $17.00 a month the second year.

Each family was provided housing and a half-acre lot where they could raise fruits and vegetables. They were to have a monthly allotment of 100 lb. bag of taro and of flour.

The life of the German immigrants making their home in Lihue, Kauai, revolved around the Lutheran Church. Its structure was prefabricated in Germany and shipped around the Horn to Lihue where it was reassembled. The German school established in Lihue was known for its excellence throughout the Kingdom of Hawaii.

On the *Ehrenfels,* one such German recruit was August Bomke, (Max's future father-in-law), born in 1837, in West Prussia and christened Johann August Bomke. Making the voyage with him were Julianne, his wife, and their six daughters and two sons. The five oldest children were from August's first marriage to Julianne's cousin, Juliana Draheim. Among these five children was Auguste Mary who later became Max's first wife. The three younger children included Therese Juliana who was three years old when they arrived in Hawaii. She later became Max's second wife and my grandmother. The family left Germany February 18, 1883, and arrived in Hawaii, May 2, 1883.

August Bomke probably didn't fit the strict category of a "worker." He had been in the Prussian army for six years and saw combat against Denmark, Austria and France. Among his injuries, he had lost three toes from frostbite. Now forty-six years old, Bomke soon became a Luna (overseer) at the Lihue Plantation on Kauai. As we would say in Hawaii, my maternal great-grandfather was "one tough bugga."

Max came to Kauai two years after the Bomke family. He went to work for the Eleele plantation, established in 1884 and later absorbed by McBride Sugar Company. Eleele had its own mill, a harbor, later known as Port Allen and an electric railway, which transported the sugar cane to the mill. Max took a special interest in the railway and soon became skilled in its maintenance and operation.

August Bomke took a special interest in Max and greatly admired the adventuresome life that had finally brought him to Kauai. He was invited often to the Bomke home. Early in 1886, Max began to court August's eighteen-year-old daughter, Auguste. She was a shy, quiet girl and had finished school in Germany. Since coming to Kauai, Auguste had stayed home and helped her stepmother, especially in caring for the younger Bomke children.

Max and Auguste were married in the Lihue Lutheran Church on September 5, 1886; he was thirty and she was nineteen. A year later, their first child, Marianne, was born at the Eleele Plantation.

Shortly thereafter, Max was offered a job involving a railroad project on the island of Hawaii. The family moved to Pahala on the Big Island. Their second daughter, Auguste was born here in 1888. About a year later, the family moved again. Max found a job with Hana Sugar Plantation located on the extreme eastern tip of the island of Maui. At this time, Auguste was expecting their third child within the next month.

Before the family settled in Hana, Auguste, along with the two small children, went home to Lihue. Here in the large Bomke household, she would have lots of care and help. Max Jr. was born in 1888 at the Bomke home. Auguste, with the three small children, joined Max shortly thereafter at their home in Hana. From all the accounts, Auguste was a strong person of sturdy German stock, but she contacted typhoid fever and died at their home in Hana on October 6, 1891. A grieving Max, with three youngsters under four years old to care for, turned to the Bomke family on Kauai. The grandparents, August and Julie, took the children to live with them. Max returned to Hana and continued with his job at the sugar plantation for several more years.

August Johann Bomke
Julianne Draheim Bomke

2

ABOUT LAYSAN ISLAND

In late 1892, George N. Wilcox, President of the North Pacific Phosphate and Fertilizer Company offered Max the job as foreman of their guano mining operation on Laysan Island. This company had been formed in 1890 and began the guano mining operation on Laysan Island that same year. After one and a half years of operation, the company was losing money and heavily in debt. Wilcox felt that the company could become profitable if it were to replace the German foreman, William Weisbarth and the work force he had brought with him from the Gilbert Islands.

During negotiations with the Kingdom of Hawaii concerning the lease of Laysan Island in 1890, Wilcox recalled hearing about a young German whaler who had attained some sort of legal rights to the Island of Laysan. This person was paid a small royalty on the profits of the mining operation on Laysan.

The only record of this fact is to be found in *The Sales Builder* for January 1939. This was a monthly publication by the Star Bulletin Printing House "for the advancement of industry, commerce and agriculture." This issue featured the history of fertilizer and the history of Pacific Guano and Fertilizer Company, commonly known as PG&F. An excerpt from this publication reads:

> He (Maximillian Schlemmer) saw Hawaii first on a whaling cruise, returned in 1885 to settle, soon took squatter possession of Laysan Island, enthusiastically boosted for exploitation of its guano deposits, and, when operations started, claimed, got, a modest royalty as "King of Laysan."…He was PG&F superintendent from 1896 to close of operations.

Wilcox learned that Max was presently employed at Hana Sugar Plantation and went there to meet with him. After a short interview with Max, Wilcox was impressed with Max's strong character, his spirit of adventure, his knowledge of guano and the ingenuity he had shown in obtaining squatter's rights to Laysan Island. Furthermore, Max was German; a fact that should please the German

Company, Hackfeld, which was the financial backer of the North Pacific Phosphate and Fertilizer Company.

It became apparent that Max had never been to Laysan Island. When he accepted the job offer from Wilcox, Max realized he must learn more about Laysan Island if he was going to live there. Much of what he learned would dispel many of the fantasies he held about living on an island paradise in the Pacific.

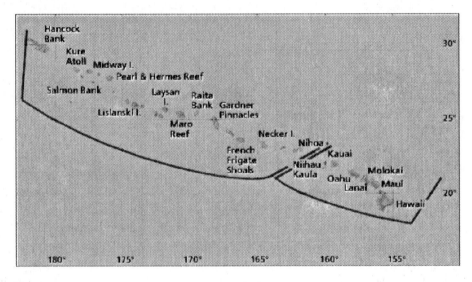

Northwest Hawaiian Islands and main islands of the state of Hawaii

Laysan was officially discovered by Captain Stanikowich aboard the Russian ship, *Moller*, on March 24, 1828. He named the Island, Moller, after his ship, not knowing the island had already been discovered and named Laysan. There appears to be no certain record of when it was first discovered and why it was named Laysan. However, according to the *Atoll Research Bulletin, No.171*, examination of logs of whaling ships in the Pacific, reveal that "the only ship listed as whaling in the Pacific prior to 1828, and with a captain named (John) Briggs, was the *Wilmington and Liverpool Packet* of New Bedford which made two voyages, on either of which Laysan may have been discovered…Briggs' discovery of Laysan must have occurred no later than 1826 and possibly as early as 1821 or 1822."

While exploring among the Pacific islands known today as the Northwest Hawaiian Islands, Captain John Paty landed on Laysan Island on May 1, 1857.

He subsequently annexed the island to the Kingdom of Hawaii. In his published account, Captain Paty describes Laysan as follows:

> Laysan Island—W. by N. ¾ N. from Honolulu 808 miles. This is a low sand island, 25 to 30 feet High; 3 miles long and 1 ½ broad.
>
> The surface is covered with beach grass, and half a dozen small palm trees were seen. It has a lagoon in the centre (salt) 1 mile long and half a mile wide, of salt water and not a hundred yards from the lagoon, an abundance of tolerable good fresh water can be had by digging two feet, and near the lagoon was found a deposit of guano. The island is "literally covered" with birds; there is, at low estimate 800,000. Seal and turtle were numerous on the beach, and might be easily taken. They were evidently unaccustomed to the sight of man, as they scarcely move at our approach, and the birds are so tame and plentiful, that it was difficult to walk about the island without stepping upon them. The gulls lay enormous large eggs, of which I have a specimen. A bank of rocks and sand extends off to the South and West 6 to 8 miles or more. Good anchorage can be found on the West side of the island in from 4 to 20 fathoms, by selecting a sandy spot to anchor upon, half to 2 miles from the beach.
>
> The best landing is about one-third of the distance from the Northern to the Southern point of the island, where there is a very smooth sand beach.

Although Laysan Island is just over 800 miles from Honolulu, it is perhaps one of the most isolated places in he world. It lies about 2,000 miles from the North American land mass as well as this same distance from the Asian continent.

Laysan is a volcanic island that erupted from the floor of the ocean some 18 million years ago. It was a lofty mountain pinnacle that was worn down over the ages to a speck of an island set atop a giant undersea mountain range. Over millions of years, this mountain range rose above the water and formed pinnacles, islets, shoals, reefs, and low sand bars slightly above the tide. It sweeps 1300 miles as a dragon's tail, northwest in the Pacific from it's beginning with Kauai, the northernmost of the main Hawaiian islands. Sometimes this group of islets, islands and shoals is called the Hawaiian Archipelago, but it is best known today as the Northwest Hawaiian Islands

Laysan is the largest of the Northwest Hawaiian Islands. It is a low-lying coral island ringed by sand dunes. Its highest point is forty feet. The island is roughly rectangular in shape. There is a saltine lagoon in the center of the island, which takes up about one-fifth of the total land area. The latitude is about the same as Monterey, Mexico and Miami, Florida.

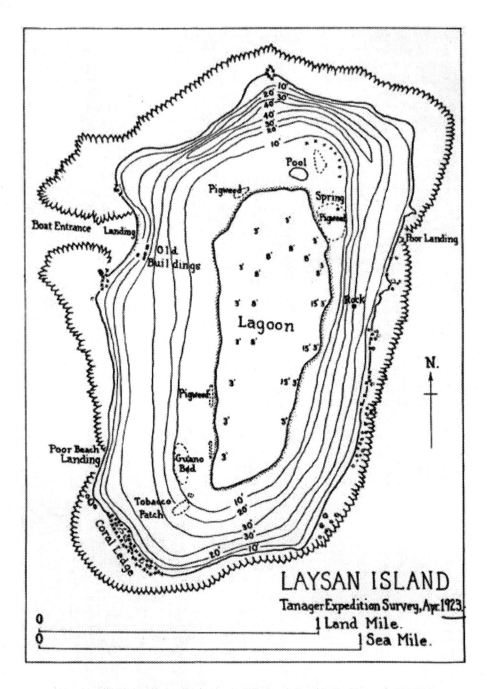

Laysan Island, principal source of fertizer for Hawaiian plantations.

Although Laysan lies outside the tropic zone, summer heat averages 90 to 100 degrees. The lack of shade trees makes it seem even warmer. Sand storms are a constant threat. Northwest winter storms thrash the island with heavy surf, rain and at times, hail.

Laysan Island has an asset not shared by others in this northwest island group. It has an abundance of fresh water. This gave rise to a unique bird population; giant seabirds living side by side with fragile land birds.

The following is an excerpt from a lecture given by Dr. Hugo Schauinsland, an eminent German scientist and professor who visited Laysan Island with his wife Adele in 1896. This lecture was masterfully translated by Miklos D. F. Udvardy of the National Museum of Natural History.

Albatross on Laysan Island

Laysan is a true bird paradise; nowhere on earth is there another place like this. The land birds occupy an inferior position, enduring their role of barely being tolerated by the seabirds who are the dominant and ruling class here. Next to the seabirds, all others take second place, and their character has a marked influence on the island. Seabirds rush here from the vast expanse of the North Pacific, to carry out their breeding duties. The island is ideally suitable for this, with its sandy soil. Many other uninhabited islands have a rocky substrate which makes them unsuitable to the shearwaters and diving birds who often require meter-deep burrows to make their nests in. Huge masses of birds come to breed here! During our arrival here when we first approached the island, we could see from quite a distance away, a veritable cloud of birds looming over the island. The flocks of storm petrels (*Haliplana fuliginosa* Peale) that were milling around in the distance, looked like a swarm of bees.

It is difficult to estimate the numbers in such a multitude. The numbers making up those bird clouds, however, were probably in the several tens of thousands, perhaps even hundreds of thousands. There are some locations on Laysan where literally every square foot of land is occupied by breeding birds.

It is virtually impossible, even for a cautious person and especially at night, to take a step without his foot endangering the birds. Moreover, the breeding birds are not only distributed *horizontally* on the island but also *vertically*, since they live not only next to one another but also over and beneath one another. There are wide expanses that are literally undermined by the burrows of the different species of shearwaters, especially where the sand is rather loose and the vegetation sparse. Nothing is more difficult than crossing such a place! The thin sandy covering over the burrows breaks through all the time, leaving you with every step to sink knee-deep with one foot, and then with the other. Where the shrub-like goosefoot forms thickets, there are not two, but four parties living above one another.

The booby and the frigate bird make their nests on top of the shrubbery. Some of the land birds prefer to nest deeper below in the branches (mostly *Acrocephalus*, but at times *Himatione*). Below them, shaded by the branches at ground level, is where the gorgeous tropical birds breed over the burrows where the black shearwaters raise their young in underground apartments. And so, with the birds living in four vertically stacked levels (stories), the comparison of these bird cities to tenement houses is easy to see. Just as a lack of enough living area forces people to build vertically and live over one another, the crowds of birds overpopulating Laysan are similarly forced into selecting available vertical space as suitable living quarters.

What an admirable drive the bird has, a drive which directs it as it flutters over a thousand miles of ocean, with an overwhelming, heartfelt compulsion to rush back to the place where its cradle once stood, in order to fulfill its parental role and duties. One is awestruck by the bird's ability to accurately schedule its arrival time, almost to within an hour; where is the compass that guides its flight through the storms and hurricanes over the vast ocean toward this tiny speck of land?

A few months later, the appearance of the island was again changed by the immigration of an even more impressive bird than the one just described. In the last days of October, the first outposts of the magnificent albatrosses appear, and a few days later, from a higher vantage point, the island looks as if it were covered by large snowflakes. There is hardly a spot from which the dazzling white plumage of an albatross does not reflect back. There are often so many of them that many must be satisfied with inferior sites, and even more are forced to move again.

Of the invasions of the other birds, I shall only mention the terns, because of the shear magnitude of their invasion. During the first few days, when most of the birds are still busy searching for a suitable nest site, the fluttering multitude of these birds cause the island to look, from a distance, as if a heavy smoke curtain lay above it.

In the late 1880's, Laysan Island became well known to a variety of interest groups. Members from the scientific community around the world visited Laysan Island to study the unique bird life, and the unique marine life. They collected specimens that even today, have a prominent place in museums. Leaders in the fast growing sugar cane industry in Hawaii, looking for a cheap source of fertilizer, became aware of the rich guano deposits on Laysan and set up mining operations. And then there were the bird pirates, coming mostly from Japan. These bird pirates ruthlessly exploited the birds for their beautiful plumage over a ten to fifteen year period.

3

A SHORT STAY IN HONOLULU

In late 1892, Max Schlemmer was offered a job by George W. Wilcox to become foreman at a guano digging operation on the island of Laysan

Max accepted the job at Laysan. However, while passing through Honolulu to visit his orphaned children at Lihue, Kauai, he decided to join the Honolulu Police Force.

Shortly after joining the force, he was promoted to the rank of Captain in their mounted police. He was assigned to Honolulu's China Town. In those days the immigrant Chinese wore their hair in braided "pony-tails" that hung down their backs. These were known as queues. These queues provided Max with an effective tool for riot control.

At the height of an opium riot, Max rounded up the ringleaders, tied their queues together and marched them to jail. Thus he put to rest a nasty situation with little or no bloodshed. For this expedient use of force in the face of dire hostility, Max received a commendation and was presented a gold watch.

Shortly after Max had received this commendation, he and his fellow officers became involved in Hawaii's most serious political crisis, the revolution of 1893. Queen Liliuokalani refused to abide by the "Bayonet Constitution" of 1887, which her late brother, King Kalakaua, had been forced to adopt.

The haole (Caucasian) planters and businessmen of The Reform Party were bent on destroying the monarchy and annexing Hawaii to the U.S. Their leader Lorrin Thurston formed the Committee of Public Safety. In a show of force, he called out the Honolulu Rifles (a secret haole militia) and installed a provisional government headed by ex-Supreme Court Justice Sanford Dole.

Max, along with the police force and soldiers, was loyal to the Queen. They were well-armed and ready to fight. However, when boat loads of U.S. sailors and marines landed to reinforce the Honolulu rifles, Queen Liliuokalani capitulated; not to the revolutionaries but to the superior forces of America.

The following day, to the complete surprise of Marshal Wilson and the rest of the police force, Max abruptly quit the police force and continued on to Kauai to visit his children.

From Kauai, Max wrote to the Marshal's office asking if they would make an effort to retrieve his watch that had been stolen prior to his departure.

The reply to Max's letter from the Marshal's office follows:

Marshal's Office

Honolulu, HI

June 20, 1893

Mr. Max Schlemmer

Kiluea Plantation, Kauai

Dear friend Max,

I received your letter last Sunday morning. I was sorry it wasn't you in its place. Somehow or another I believed you would return. Not only I, but also the old man. He asked me first thing Sunday morning if you had shown up. Your Lieutenant was made captain somehow or another. It's strange Klemme couldn't get there.

Up until now, your horse has not appeared. I forwarded one letter to you the other day, from Maui.

Well, Max, I hope you are satisfied in your new job. The boys are all sorry of your departure. As far as they, or even the old man are concerned, you could come back and get your Captaincy anytime. I will close now, hoping to hear from you often. The boys all send their "Aloha Nui."

I remain yours sincerely,

Captain H A Yuen
Honolulu, Hawaii

P.S. About that watch that was stolen up there. We will keep an eye open for it.

Maxmillian Schlemmer

Police Captain, Island of Oahu
Kingdom of Hawaii 1893

In mid-summer, 1893, Max visited with his children in Lihue and spent most of his time with the Bomke family. Therese Juliana, Auguste's half sister had become a "little mother" to Mary, Gussie and Max Jr. Therese cared for the three children most of the time and they adored her. She seemed mature for her age, with a healthy dose of common sense and a no-nonsense attitude.

Max soon realized that he loved Therese as the children did. He proposed marriage. Therese accepted and agreed to wait for his return from Laysan Island. Max planned to get started with his new job in the guano mining operation on Laysan before bringing a bride and his three children to live there.

4

MAX ARRIVES ON LAYSAN

It was late summer, 1893, when Max finally arrived on Laysan as foreman of the guano digging operation. The North Pacific Phosphate and Fertilizer Company had hired him. This company had been formed in 1890 when George D. Freeth and George N. Wilcox persuaded H. Hackfeld and Company, a German company in Honolulu, to finance their company, which was to mine the guano deposit on Laysan Island.

Freeth was an Englishman who had sailed from Honolulu to Laysan Island in February 1890. It was reported in *The Friend*, April 1890, that he had taken possession of the island, hoisted the Hawaiian flag, and left two men there to hold possession.

On 13 March, he returned to Honolulu and reported that there were good guano deposits on the island. He knew George Wilcox only slightly, and knew that he had at one time, managed a guano operation on Jarvis Island. In mid 1890, the two men got together and formed a business partnership. They were able to get the Hawaiian Kingdom to grant them the right to mine guano deposits on Laysan and Lisiansky Islands for a period of 20 years.

Freeth was appointed general manager for the operation and was to live on the island. With this appointment, he was given the title of "Governor of Laysan and Lisiansky Islands." With supplies and equipment, a foreman and eight laborers aboard, he sailed on the *S.S. Pele* for Laysan Island in November 1890.

After only part of the cargo had been landed, the party was driven from the island by one of the notorious winter storms, common to the area at this time of year. They returned to Honolulu; it was late December before they were able to land successfully on Laysan. The guano digging operation began in early 1891.

In April 1891, the first shipment of guano, 80 tons, was sold in Honolulu at $50 a ton. By November 30, 1891, the company had shipped 1,017 tons of guano to Europe, 200 tons to California and 200 tons to Hawaii. But it soon became apparent that this was not a profitable operation. The company was $39,949.91 in the red.

In November 1892, the Hackfeld Co. chartered the schooner *Liholiho* and hired Dr. W. Averdam, a noted German chemist. His mission was to determine if the mining of guano on Laysan Island could become a profitable operation. Dr. Averdam returned with the recommendation that the guano operation on Laysan should be shut down and that a modern chemical fertilizer plant be built in Honolulu. It would be some years before H. Hackfeld and Co. acted on this recommendation.

When Freeth established the guano operation on Laysan, he hired laborers and their foreman, Captain William Weisbarth, from the Gilbert Islands. (Today these islands are known as the Republic of Kiribati.)

Weisbarth was a somewhat arrogant German married to a native woman from the Gilbert Islands. He was a swarthy, stout barrel of a man with short clipped hair and mustache. His dress was a gaudy pair of striped pajamas. It seems that striped pajamas were the royal garb of the King of the Gilbert Islands.

Robert Louis Stevenson, in his book, *A Tale of Tapu,* writes that while visiting Makin in the Gilbert Islands, "The King was there in striped pajamas."

Although Weisbarth, in his royal garb, seemed to be doing a good job, his boss, Captain George Freeth, together with George N. Wilcox, president of the company, decided the Pilipati, as they were known to the Hawaiians, were to be replaced by laborers from Japan. Further, Max Schlemmer would replace Captain William Weisbarth. As could be expected, this situation created much animosity between the two Germans.

Weisbarth left Laysan Island but remained in Hawaii. With his schooner, *Lavinia,* he hauled cargo between the Hawaiian Islands. Sometimes he had a guano shipment from Laysan. Whenever the two Germans met, an explosive argument was sure to ensue. Until the day William Weisbarth left Hawaii, he was Max Schlemmer's nemesis.

Laysan was fast becoming a "guano island." A Captain of one of the schooners chartered to take the guano to Honolulu gives a detailed description of guano operations as follows:

> Laborers mined the guano, consisting mostly of a hard, conglomerated, phosphate of lime, with picks, crowbars, shovels and sledges. This material was placed on cars on the narrow gauge railway and pulled by mules to storage sheds where the guano was kept until a ship arrived. A small amount of brown guano (bird droppings and soil) was also collected and sifted, but it was a small proportion of the total amount of guano shipped from the island.

When ships came in, the guano was carried from the storage sheds in barrows holding about a ton out onto the wharf that extended from the west side of the island. At the end of the wharf the guano was dumped into a chute, which deposited the material into lighters. These lighters in turn transferred their cargo to the clipper ships that were anchored between two buoys off shore. As much as 100 to 125 tons per day could be loaded under favorable conditions.

Captain William Weisbarth and Dr. W. Averdam
conferring about the guano mining operation.

The guano-shipping period lasted only from April through September. If ships arrived during times of high surf, a "winter landing" was possible on the north coast of the island. During the early days of the guano operation, only a caretaker remained on the island during the winter months.

Once Max established his home on Laysan, he and his family usually remained there the year round.

Loading guano from the dock at Laysan Island 1892.
Photo from Collection of J.J. Williams, at Bishop Museum

At the same time, the economics of Laysan's fledging guano industry was of no interest to the natural scientists throughout the world. Laysan's true value lay in its pristine ecosystem. Because of the presence of fresh water on Laysan and because of its extreme isolation in the Pacific, the discovery of land birds existing among a multitude of seabirds was of particular interest to the scientific community.

During the 1890's, a number of scientific collecting expeditions were carried out. The first, most extensive expedition was one sponsored by Walter Rothschild in 1891. During their visit on Laysan Island, conditions were recorded and a biological survey made. They collected numerous birds, including four species new to science.

Henry Palmer, leader of the expedition, declared that Laysan was the "greatest bird island in the world."

It should be noted that during the years Max lived on the island, he collected a small number of birds. Records exist that show 39 specimens of 9 species. All but two of these specimens are now housed in the Museum of Comparative Zoology, Harvard. He also collected a small number of fish specimen.

After receiving "a fine collection of nests and eggs," William Y. Bingham wrote to Max, on Bishop Museum stationery, "I am directed by a vote of the Trustees of the Bernice Pauahi Bishop Museum, to acknowledge the receipt of your Gift to the Museum, and to return to you their thanks for the same."

5

THE LONELY BRIDE HAS A VISITOR

Max and Therese were married on March 22, 1895, in the Lihue Lutheran Church. Max was thirty-eight. Therese was not quite sixteen. They sailed to Laysan Island on their honeymoon, accompanied by Max's three children who were Therese's nieces and nephew that she had been raising: Marianne (now called Mary), age 8, Gussie, age 7 and Max Jr., age 5.

They were greeted by dismal and meager surroundings; a wretched little mining camp that had sprung up to house laborers from Japan. A narrow rail track ran from the guano fields to the dock. A stalwart mule drew carts along the track. Several other animals were on the island, including a milk cow. It died suddenly. A feather ball was found stuck in its gullet.

Their quarters had a kerosene stove and a few wicker chairs, Pots and pans and work clothes hung about. Quilts and cots to sleep on were in another room. Insects of various sizes were everywhere. A hurricane lamp sat on a table in the corner of the entry room with old copies of newspapers: *The Friend, Honolulu Commercial Advertiser,* and *The Honolulu Star.*

As night fell, the glow of the sunset was replaced by the reflection of their oil lamp on the walls of their hovel. From among the Japanese laborers, a cook was provided for the family.

The young bride had never expected a honeymoon nor a mansion. She was bewildered but not disappointed. In these strange surroundings, Therese had difficulty sleeping. The birdcalls at night were disturbing and frightening, especially that of the Black Shearwater. They would emit horrible cries much as a human lamenting a terrible tragedy.

It was especially difficult to wander about at night without stepping through a nest. Birds were so numerous, they built their nests vertically one atop the other. Still, there was not enough space on the island for the birds to breed.

The Schlemmer's home and lighthouse at Laysan Island

Huge masses of birds would approach the island from the sea like a cloud on the horizon. As their breeding cycle ended, another mass of birds would arrive. It was a breeding cycle that was developed over thousands of years, the timing of which would rival Japan's train schedules today.

The feeling of isolation was quite intense. There was no "pony express" that came on a regular schedule to bring mail, medical supplies, provisions, supplies and the like. Perhaps two or three ships per month stopped at Laysan, stopping only if the ship's captain decided to do so, depending somewhat on wind, weather and other conditions. It was a 6 to 8 day trip to Honolulu. Growing a garden was impossible. Often, a ship would surprise them with a gift of fresh fruits and vegetables.

The Black-footed Albatross eggs were preserved by the barrel.

Ottilie and friends with a collection of Albatross eggs.

One visitor found them "fresh and also very palatable if allowed to remain in boiling water for twenty-five minutes. In fact, they had a much better flavor than the similar product from the hen."

Therese was overwhelmed by the harsh atmosphere. Added to an already difficult adjustment, she and Max were further distressed and saddened by the loss of their son Adam, at birth. However, the gloom that hung so heavy about Max and Therese began to lift when they received word that Hackfeld and Company was sending their flagship to Laysan. Aboard was one of Germany's most eminent scientists, Dr. Hugo H. Schauinsland and his wife Adele.

At last Max's young bride would be able to enjoy the company of another woman. The Doctor and his wife set up their laboratory and workshop next to the Laysan lighthouse. They proceeded to process, label, and pack 15 trunks of specimens from land and sea.

Busy as she was, Adele found time to visit with the lonely bride Therese. They became fast friends and corresponded until the outbreak of World War I. Eric Schlemmer, my uncle, kept two of these letters.

Before the Shauninsland's departed from Laysan Island, Max presented the Doctor with the remains of a Hawaiian Monk Seal. When the Doctor presented this animal to science, it was declared a new species and today bears his name: Monachus Schauinslands.

It must be noted that during the fifteen years Max spent on Laysan, he had rarely seen a Monk Seal. He had, however, discovered one of their skeletal remains and preserved it. Seals had been slaughtered almost to the point of extinction. Much like whales, they were slaughtered for their skins and oil. When the Hawaiian bark *Gambia* docked at Honolulu in 1859, 1500 sealskins and 240 barrels of oil were aboard. With the coming of the 20th century, petroleum reduced the need for whale and seal oil. The age of the sea hunters ended.

Although few in number, the Hawaiian Monk Seal continues to exist in the Northwest Hawaiian waters. It is the rarest mammal in the world and has a most unusual feature; it sheds its skin like a reptile. Were it not for Max Schlemmer and Dr. Shauinsland, the Hawaiian Monk Seal might have disappeared from the face of the earth.

The time had now come for the Schauinslands to leave the island. From the Doctor's journal we have an excellent description of their departure from Laysan Island:

> It was now September and darkness came early. Along with the beginning winter months, came the wild northwest storms. The proud ship *Hackfeld* arrived only to be forced to tack back and forth in front of Laysan in boiling seas in an attempt to retrieve my wife and me.
>
> On the third day, the Captain succeeded in maneuvering the ship into a safe spot where he dropped anchor. The weather did not improve. A mighty Western swell caused the ship to roll so much that its yardarms almost touched the water. On the evening of September 22, word reached shore from the ship that we must board at once. The ship needed to sail immediately before the masts were ruined in the extreme rolling action of the ship.
>
> We rushed to get ready. After bidding a hasty farewell to Max and his family, we departed for the ship in a small boat. As the last rays of the sun set over the island, we climbed a rope ladder up the side of the violently rolling ship. It was an experience we prayed we would never have to repeat. Unfortunately, our departure was again delayed. The storm passed and the wind died completely. We were forced to sit there for two more days. We were seasick as the ship rolled lazily in the dead calm. Sleep was impossible. Then, on the third

day, a favorable trade wind sprang up. The ship's lines were released from the buoys, the anchor was raised and the ship sailed away from the menacing reef.

The Hawaiian Monk Seal Shown here on South Point Laysan Island in 1923.
It is considered to be the rarest mammal in the world.

From atop the Laysan lighthouse, Max dipped the flag in a farewell salute as Therese waved a sad goodbye. At the ship's rail, the Schauinslands watched as the two solitary figures faded from view. They now understood the kind of courage it took to stay in solitude for six to eight months totally separated from the rest of the world.

6

MAX ESTABLISHED AS "KING OF LAYSAN ISLAND"

After the death of Adam, Max had a trying time dealing with the fact that he had brought his family to such a God-forsaken place. He envisioned other tragedies that could lie ahead. His confidence had been shattered with Adam's death. Could he successfully bring more children into the world?

He wondered aloud if his efforts on the island were appreciated by Hackfeld. Why had he not been appraised of the fertilizer plant they were building on Oahu?

Max was working himself to the point of exhaustion in an effort to forget the loss of their child and the job insecurity he was beginning to feel. He was also gravely concerned about Therese and their second child she was expecting soon.

Meanwhile, a ship, the *C.D.Bryant*, stood offshore for thirteen days, taking on 1100 tons of guano for the H. Hackfeld Company in Honolulu. During this time, the ship's captain, A.J. Simpson, spent some of each day visiting and talking with Max. He soon became aware of Max's struggles and concerns about his job and life for his family on the island.

Captain Simpson decided that the company would best be served in the long run if Max and his family were to take a vacation to Kauai. They could stay with Therese's parents, the Bomkes. And he had just the man to leave on Laysan, August Toeller who had been brought to Laysan to man the ship's launch. He was now to be in charge on Laysan during the absence of Max.

On June 11th, while Hawaii commemorated the birth of Kamehameha the Great, Max and Therese welcomed my mother into the world on Laysan Island; Ottilie Laysan Schlemmer. Ottilie's birth gave Max a new lease on life. Now, with the birth of a healthy child, his confidence was restored. Shortly after my Mother's birth, Max and his family left for Kauai.

The Max Schlemmer family 1898. The infant is my mother, Ottilie with her half siblings: Max, Mary and Gussie.

Mother was baptized Ottilie Laysan Schlemmer, August 16, 1897 by Pastor Hans Isenberg at the German Lutheran Church at Lihue, Kauai.

The Schlemmer family returned to Laysan and were most grateful for the help August Toeller had given them. He had been a good manager during Max's absence. But he had also proved to be a strong and compassionate person whom they had needed to see them through one of the most trying times of their lives. He stayed on for about six months; then returned to his home in Washington State.

After Toeller's departure, Max returned to his job with renewed vigor. His enthusiasm soon waned however, due to the behavior of Captain Spencer, the company's manager for the island.

Often Spencer displayed a menacing attitude toward the Japanese workers. This made it difficult for Max to do his job.

By 1899, Max's distrust of the Captain had grown to the point where he had to do something.

BAYVIEW SALOON with Max, Therese, family and friends.

In addition to the growing animosity between Max and Captain Spencer, Max worried again about the wisdom of raising a family on Laysan Island. A second child was soon to be born. Max could no longer see raising a family at Laysan under present conditions. He decided to leave Laysan Island.

The Schlemmer family moved to Kauai in late 1899. Another daughter, Therese Julia, was born, January 13, 1900 in Waimea.

With the financial backing of his father-in-law, August Bomke, Max opened the Bayview Saloon and Billiard Parlor in Waimea.

Since Max had become a businessman in the Territory of Hawaii, which was now part of the United States, he decided it was fitting and proper that he should become a U.S. citizen. In September 1900, Max appeared at the Circuit Court of the Fifth Judicial Circuit of the Territory of Hawaii and received his papers that declared him a citizen of the United States of America. They were signed by Judge Gilbert F. Little and Harry D. Wishard, Clerk of the Court. Max carried these papers wherever he went and displayed them to whomever he thought might be interested in his newfound glory as an American citizen.

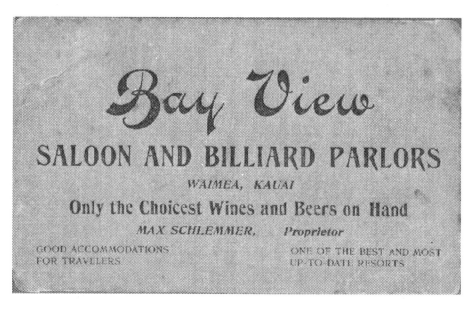

Max's Business Card

Bayview Saloon decorated for the holidays

At about the time Max was becoming a citizen in Honolulu, violence was breaking out at Laysan Island. Although this news came as no great surprise, the level of violence disturbed him a great deal.

On August 11, 1900, a bloody riot took place on Laysan. The Japanese laborers rebelled against the overseers of the guano mining, demanding better working conditions and increased wages.

On September 8, 1900, headlines from the *Pacific Commercial Advertiser* read, "Laysan Island's Story of Blood." The following is an excerpt from the article:

> War had been declared, waged, and ended on Laysan Island. Four against forty: those were the odds. Four white men fighting desperately against forty infuriated Japanese. And the white men conquered. On the evening of Saturday, 11 August 1900, The forty Japanese rose in a body, determined to annihilate all the white people and run things to suit themselves. Captain Spencer, the manager of the bird guano mining operation, called his son and Captain Spilner, late of the Honolulu Mounted Patrol, and the engineer Luhrs together. They went out to talk to the mob, which had gathered between the white men's house and the Japanese quarters. Captain Spencer asked what the trouble was, whereupon the leaders of the mob answered defiantly. Cursing and shouting, they threatened the white men's lives. They carried flags and were waving them excitedly. They were armed with knives, stones, clubs, and cutlasses made of sharpened hoop iron. They made a movement toward the platform and old Captain Spencer raised a six-shooter in either hand. "The first man who steps up onto this platform shall die!" shouted Captain Spencer. "Shoot away!" cried the mob. At the signal from their leader, they charged all together for the platform. Though they moved quickly, Captain Spencer's trigger finger moved quicker. Eight times his revolvers spoke and they spoke to the point. The pistols in the hands of the other white men also had something to say. Two of the Japanese leaders dropped dead. Three others fell helpless, sorely wounded.

The following day, the 39 surviving Japanese were rounded up at gunpoint and taken prisoner aboard the *Ceylon*. The two dead Japanese were buried. On August 16, the *Ceylon* set sail for Honolulu with Spencer and Spilner aboard, along with the Japanese. The ship arrived in Honolulu on Sept 7. Spencer and Spilner were arrested by police and questioned.

After a ten-day trial, it became obvious that it was difficult to determine who did the actual killing. As a result, all charges against Spencer and Spilner were dropped. In the final analysis, there was reason to believe Spilner was the culprit. It was known he held a deep-seated hatred for the Japanese. Although during the trial he testified he fired one shot into the air, and one into the house, Spencer later testified that Spilner had told him after the incident, "My two shots counted alright. They got their man."

It was a time of quiet crisis on Laysan. Except for the bird activity; the landing and taking off of 17 varieties of about two million birds, Laysan Island lay like a beached whale. Who would, or could, go out there and bring the island back to life, or at least shut down the guano mining operation in an orderly fashion?

These were the questions raised at an emergency meeting of the company that had now changed from North Pacific Phosphate and Fertilizer to Pacific Guano and Fertilizer Company.

The unanimous choice was Max Schlemmer. The powers-to-be were well acquainted with Max's history on the island. Earlier he had acquired squatter's rights to the island and claimed a small royalty from the sale of guano to Pacific Guano and Fertilizer Company. Though this royalty was small, Max's ego was large. The royalty was to be paid to Maximilian Schlemmer, King of Laysan. His title was usually Captain Schlemmer, and this was correct; not only for his rank as Captain on the Honolulu Police Force, but also for being a Captain of sailing vessels.

The newspapers in Hawaii picked up on his title of "King of Laysan" and never dropped it. When writing about Max on a routine subject, he was given the title "Captain." When he was involved in an event that could be parlayed into something sensational, he was "The King of Laysan."

The *Pacific Commercial Advertiser* never missed a beat when it was announced that Max Schlemmer would be sent to Laysan as the new manager. Following up on their story of the bloody incident on Laysan, they implied that no person other than one with the stature of a King would be sent to ease troubles on that island.

The *Pacific Commercial Advertiser* article, dated September 20, 1900, read:

> There is to be a King on Laysan Island. Max Schlemmer will go there and become monarch of all he surveys. Captain Joseph Spencer, the former ruler of that interesting little spot will not return to Laysan. Schlemmer has been to Laysan before. He will return to manage affairs for the Pacific Guano and Fertilizer Co. He will take along with him a new party of Japanese laborers to work the guano. He expects to set sail in a few days on the bark *Ceylon*, which will carry a large quantity of stores and supplies for the island. Before Capt. Spencer took charge of Laysan, Schlemmer was superintendent there for five or six years. For the past few years he has been conducting a hotel and saloon at Waimea on Kaui. He returned to Honolulu last week and was re-engaged by the fertilizer company to look after their interests on the little island. There is still a large quantity of guano left on Laysan Island, enough to last for several

years to come. It is expected that the schooner *Aloha*, which left for Laysan several weeks ago, will return to Honolulu any day unless its Captain Frey decides to stay on the island until more laborers are sent from here.

King Max with his family, set sail for Laysan Island in the early part of October. He was also bringing along a new Japanese work force. But it was not a good time of year to venture into the Northwest Pacific. Powerful seas churned and huge waves crashed into Laysan and other small atolls.

Max bided his time offshore on the schooner *Aloha*. As the tide subsided, the workers slipped their light boats through the sandy inlet and unloaded supplies that were to last six months.

Meanwhile chemical fertilizer was being produced on Oahu. However it was agreed that guano would continue to be received from Laysan Island until such a time as Pacific Guano and Fertilizer Co. decided what to do with that bothersome little piece of real estate.

Once again, the population on Laysan was increased when the Schlemmer's welcomed their third daughter, Ida Anna. She was born on the 1st of June, 1901.

On September 14th, America was shocked by the assassination of President McKinley. His Vice President Theodore Roosevelt took over the reins of government. Even tiny Laysan Island would be affected by the new president's micromanagement of the island's ecology.

The following year, the *USS Albatross* appeared offshore at Laysan. It was commanded by Captain Chauncey Thomas. He had been hired by the U.S. Commission of Fish and Fisheries to land a party of scientists on Laysan for the purpose of making a general biological survey of the island and to collect a variety of specimens.

When Max was notified that the *Albatross* was to visit Laysan, he sent word to the Commander that he would arrange to have the ship piloted to a safe landing.

His offer was accepted. When the *Albatross* approached Laysan through poorly chartered waters, Max dispatched a skiff and brought her safely in. Several hand written notes from Commander Thomas to Max attest to a close relationship between the two.

In one especially chatty letter, Thomas related to Max that Professor Nutting had told him of Max's patriotic feelings regarding the American flag and how those feelings were much appreciated. The Commander went on to explain, "In our service we hoist our colors in port at 8 o'clock in the morning. The Army hoists them at sunrise."

The scientific party that landed at Laysan from the *Albatross* was headed by Charles H. Gilbert of Stanford University. Also from Stanford were Walter K. Fisher and John O. Snyder. Iowa State sent Charles C. Nutting. Fisher and Snyder spent eight days as guests of Max Schlemmer, who assisted them whenever necessary.

Fisher's report, published in 1903, was of immense value as a basis of comparison with regard to the drastic changes in bird populations that occurred in the next twenty years.

As the *Albatross* prepared for its departure Max received the following hand written note from the Skipper:

Dear Sir,

We will sail at 6:30 this evening. If you have any commands for Honolulu or any letters, please do not hesitate to let me have them. I wish to express my personal and official thanks for the many courtesies you have shown me and all attached to the ship. It would have been hard to accomplish all we have been able to but for your kind assistance. Good Bye.

Very sincerely yours,

Chauncy Thomas
Commander, U.S. Navy

A second note was received by Max the same day, once again from the Skipper.

Dear Mr. Schlemmer,

Will you accept the accompanying box of cigars and smoke them with a memory of Mrs. Thomas' pleasure in all the pretty things you gave her.

Sincerely yours,

Chauncey Thomas

For Max, the box of cigars was a good beginning but he was after more. He wanted to be appointed warden for the islands of Laysan and Lisianski with police powers to protect the birds as well as advance his own interests. He was in effect collecting IOU's from people in authority from whom he would be requesting letters of recommendation at the appropriate time.

After the departure of the *Albatross*, scores of scientific expeditions continued to visit Laysan. The many specimens collected can be found in major American museums. Others were exchanged to foreign museums, while an unknown number are in private collections.

On July 3, 1902, disaster struck when his main carrier the *Ceylon* was caught in heavy weather ten days out of Laysan, and began to leak badly. The ship was abandoned and soon sank with a full load of guano aboard. It took four days for the officers and crew to return to Laysan in two small boats.

Another problem now arose to add to Max's woes. The management at Pacific Guano and Fertilizer Co., had dispatched Count A. Von Graevemeyer to assist Max Schlemmer.

It soon became obvious however, that the Count was not at Laysan to assist, but rather to take command and rule the island. Max told the Count his presence was not needed nor wanted on the island, and that he must leave at once. The Count refused and a heated argument took place while the Count was astride his horse.

Max grabbed the horse's reigns and with a solid blow to the Count's body, knocked the proud German unceremoniously to the ground.

Von Graevemeyer brought suit against Max for injury to his person and character. He demanded $5,000 dollars, a sum unheard of in the courts of Hawaii. During the trial in Honolulu, Max pleaded guilty and made a brief statement to the court. He denied kicking the Count, but admitted to striking him and unhorsing the wearer of the Iron Cross.

Judge Wilcox warned the defendant against violence, but admitted that the history of the island showed the necessity of a determined spirit to rule it. Still, it was not right for the "King" to hit the Count. The matter was ended with Max being fined $10 dollars.

After the Graevemeyer incident, Max had time to focus on operational problems on the island. First and most important, he was confronted with how he was to ship guano to Honolulu after the loss of the *Ceylon*. Unfortunately there was no choice other than to charter ships for that purpose, further adding to losses to PG&F.

In spite of the financial difficulties of the guano mining operation on Laysan, the baby boom continued with the birth of the Schlemmer's fourth child. A son Eric Laysan Schlemmer, the little "Prince," was born on Laysan, March 22, 1903.

Therese became very busy with her brood of growing youngsters. Besides her own four children there were her stepchildren, Mary, Gussie and Max Jr. Mary and Gussie were old enough to help, especially with the babies. There were also a Japanese cook and a Japanese houseboy who helped with household chores and laundry.

The children spent many hours of the day playing along the sandy beaches. Part of the memorabilia I grew up with in our house, was a prominently displayed jar of seashells which Mother had gathered on Laysan's beaches.

My Mother told me stories about playing in the ocean. Even though the little ones stayed near the shore, her mother tied a rope around each child's waist. She did this in the event a shark appeared nearby. Therese could "reel" the children in quickly. My grandmother discovered that the albumin of the gooney bird egg whites was a wonderful shampoo.

Max wrote in his journal about the baby bird with one leg he found near a work shed. He took the bird home and the family cared for it until it could fly and "hop along" on its own. The bird became a family pet and Max's constant companion. It followed him everywhere he went.

In 1903, a little over a hundred miles north, at the island of Midway, the Trans Pacific cable was laid connecting Hawaii to the Far East. The cable from Midway was the final link in a worldwide communication system.

On July 4, 1903, President Teddy Roosevelt celebrated America's independence by sending a message around the globe in nine and one half minutes from his mansion in Oyster Bay, N.Y. to Governor Taft in the Philippines.

Now that the cable company had been established on Midway, Max decided to purchase a ship the next year and start a mail and cargo route to serve both his needs on Laysan and the cable company's on Midway.

By September the mining season was over at Laysan. The *Pacific Commercial Advertiser* noted the arrival of the ship *Robert Lewis* in Honolulu where she discharged her last load of guano for the season.

The ship also brought back Max Schlemmer, "The King of Laysan" with his family. With his growing family the King could never afford any down time. During this off-season, the family lived in Honolulu. Max went to work for the Honolulu Rapid Transit Company as a motorman.

As guano deposits on Laysan began to dwindle, Max, always the entrepreneur, spent much thoughtful time trying to devise schemes whereby he could make a living on the island for himself and his family.

Max enjoyed life on Laysan. Its solitude afforded him a medium for his thoughts to roam free. He was fascinated by the royal title the newspapers in

Honolulu had conveyed upon him. He would lose it all if he abdicated his throne on Laysan and became exiled to Honolulu.

In March 1904, the *Sunday Advertiser* announced that Max Schlemmer had applied for leases of Necker and Gardiner Islands. He offered $25 dollars a year rent for each island on a 21-year lease. This sent the phones ringing in Commissioner J.W. Pratt's Territorial Land Office. Among the callers was John N. Cobb, Commissioner of the Fisheries Bureau of the U.S. Dept. of Commerce and Labor, Washington D.C. He was curious to know what species of fish Mr. Schlemmer wished to catch in the vicinity of the aforementioned islands.

Max's request had thrust Pratt into "uncharted waters." There he thrashed about a bit before coming up with some answers. First, the Territory of Hawaii must establish jurisdiction over the islands. Second, it had to be determined if the U.S. had surveyed them. Then, once leaseholds were available, they would be put up for public auction with stipulations covering modes of fishing, the protection of birds, and such things.

This was all too complicated for Max, and he abandoned his plan. He couldn't understand why others could not be a "straight shooter" like himself.

Max as a motorman for the Honolulu Rapid Transit Company, 1903.

7

MAX THE ENTREPRENEUR

By the latter part of April, there were subtle indications in the press that the Hackfeld Co., was about to take over the Pacific Guano and Fertilizer Co., (formerly the North Pacific Phosphate and Fertilizer Co.) Hackfeld had financed the company with George Wilcox as President, but the operation on Laysan was a dismal failure, and continued to lose money.

Not only was it an economic disaster, but it was an embarrassment. The crowd along Merchant Street referred to it as "Wilcox's folly." Workers on the island had rebelled and their manager was brought to trial for murder. The next manager was also brought to trial, for assaulting a Count of the German Empire. The H. Hackfeld Co. was a prominent member of the emerging Big Five sugar factors in Hawaii. As a German company, its board of directors was not about to be involved in a controversy over a small, isolated, useless piece of bird infested real estate.

On April 27, 1904, Hackfeld instructed Pacific Guano and Fertilizer Co. to sell everything except the buildings on Laysan to Max Schlemmer. A memo of that agreement of May 6, 1904 read in part: "Pacific Guano and Fertilizer Co., agrees to sell all of its boats, tools, supplies, railroad track, anchors, chains, etc, located on said Island of Laysan for the sum of $1,750.00 U.S. gold coin to Max Schlemmer."

On the same date, Max received an Agent's Commission. This gave him a license to act for Pacific Guano and Fertilizer Co., within terms of the contract and lease, which the company had with the Hawaiian Government. This authority covered both Laysan and Lisianski Islands.

With this document and bill of sale, the King of Laysan was certain all rights and powers what-so-ever on Laysan Island had been bestowed unto him. To this, the temporal powers in Hawaii and Washington D.C. looked askance. They tried to keep his conduct under close surveillance. But this proved to be a difficult task.

The "King" envisioned Laysan to be his castle and remote fortress, with a hazardous reef as its rampart. This rampart was surrounded by a mote of wild ocean. For watch dogs at the gates there were the wild, unpredictable storms that could attack at any time. However, the King also had to be aware of his foreign enemies. These enemies were bird pirates from Japan, who had been raiding these northernmost Hawaiian Islands including Laysan and Lisianski.

A skipper of a bird pirating operation could become wealthy beyond his wildest dreams. The birds were literally worth their weight in gold. After the birds were killed, their feathers and parts were preserved for shipment to such fashion centers as London, Paris and New York. It was all the rage for ladies to wear hats adorned with bird wings, feathers, and in some cases, bird breasts. Max was very much aware of the value of these wild birds.

Once Max gained control of Laysan Island, Captain William Weisbarth, Max's old nemesis, appeared on the scene. He began making overtures to Max regarding a business partnership. After much discussion, a deal was struck; Max would give to the partnership, a share in his rights on Laysan Island to include the railway, moorings, the wharf, steam launches and such. All this was valued at $5000.00.

Weisbarth was to contribute his schooner, *Lavinia*, valued at $1000.00. Max would now have the means to haul his guano cargo to Honolulu. Two-thirds of the expense of the partnership were to be borne by Schlemmer; one-third by Weisbarth. The profits were to be apportioned at the same ratio. The agreement was due to be signed at a later date. This never happened.

Up to the time of the arrival of the guano diggers on Laysan, the extent of the bird pirating was unknown. But Max knew that this was going on, especially on Lisianski Island. On May 14, 1904, Max wrote a letter to E.R. Stackable, U.S. Collector of Customs. He called attention to the fact that an unauthorized encampment of Japanese was on the island of Lisianski, a U.S. possession.

Max's concern was probably not so much prompted by a wish to report foreign encroachment on a U.S. possession, but rather by his wish to protect any business interest he might have in the future. Stackable responded to the letter and forwarded the complaint to the U.S. Secretary of Treasury.

A month later, the Coast Guard cutter *Thetis* was dispatched to Midway with supplies for the garrison of Marines that had been established to protect the cable company personnel against marauders. After discharging its cargo at Midway, the *Thetis* headed for Lisianski. There it captured 77 Japanese who were hastily taken aboard, leaving behind the priceless catch of dead birds.

Word of the abandoned booty soon reached Captain Weisbarth, the skipper of the *Lavinia*. Even though Weisbarth and Schlemmer had a tentative agreement to become business partners on Laysan Island, the birds left behind by the Coast Guard proved too much of a temptation for Weisbarth.

He left word with Max's wife Therese that he was no longer partners with her husband. He was on his way to Lisianski to retrieve the abandoned birds and take them to Nova Scotia. There he would sell them and become a rich man. Unknown to Weisbarth, the *Tangi Maru* was racing toward Lisianski to recover the same precious loot. It is believed the Japanese won the race and took the prize.

Now that Weisbarth and his ship, the *Lavinia*, had deserted him, Max was without a means of transportation for his enterprise on Laysan Island. Once all guano had been mined from Laysan, his plans were to work the guano on Lisianski and establish a shipping route that would link Laysan, Lisianski and Midway with the main port of Honolulu.

It was apparent the Marines would remain at Midway for a long time. Heavy guns had been put in place and a lighthouse built on Sand Island. The Marine garrison and cable company personnel had to be supplied and the King had plans to do just that once he acquired his flagship.

In the fall of 1904, Max took passage aboard the *Robert Lewis* for Port Townsend, Washington. There he purchased the schooner *C. Kennedy* in Seattle. Soon after his arrival at Port Townsend, news began to filter back to the local press in Honolulu regarding the marvelous exploits of Max Schlemmer. The following article was from the *Times Special Service*, Port Townsend, Washington dated Monday, Oct. 31, 1904:

> It falls to the lot of but a few mortals to be styled Kings or Governors of island domains, but such is the good fortune of Max Schlemmer, who arrived in this city recently as a passenger on the American schooner *Robert Lewis*. Mr. Schelmmer, or Gov. Schelmmer as he is known in the little group of islands where he handles the reins of government to suit his own fancy, is German by birth, but American by adoption. More than twenty years ago he left the Pacific Coast for Honolulu, seeking to make a competency for himself. He remained there for some years, working at many things, until he became an employee of the Pacific Guano and Fertilizer Co, which has a lease on the Laysan group of islands from the Hawaiian government. The Laysan group lies 900 miles northwest from Honolulu and 300 miles distant from Midway Island. There are three islands in the group and the formation is coral. The annual output of guano from Gov. Schlemmer's domain amounts to 45,000 tons. It is shipped in vessels chartered for this purpose to Honolulu where the

guano is used as fertilizer on the sugar plantations. As the stuff brings in from $55 to $60 per ton, the profit can well be imagined. The cost of transportation amounts to less than $5 a ton and labor is cheap.

The feathered inhabitants of the islands are numbered by the thousands. They furnish down to Gov. Schlemmer and his family, but he never allows any wanton killing of the birds. Eggs there are without number according to Gov. Schlemmer, they are even more palatable than the chicken variety. They constitute a goodly portion of the rations of those on the island. The last time eggs were gathered, 6,000 of them were secured by the men in three hours. They were salted to prevent spoiling. Gov. Schlemmer has no palace, no uniformed staff officials, and neither Army nor Navy. Despite all this he gets along charmingly. He is a married man and his wife and seven children reside with him in this lonely island group. He has a comfortable residence of large dimensions, no lack of servants, and lives in style becoming a ruler, albeit a small one. His subject's number but 100, and they are all under his supervision and his pay as his laborers in the guano deposits. They are all coolies from the Orient. There is not a single white person on the three islands aside from the Gov. and his family. Schlemmer is now a rich man, although no one would ever know it from his appearance, talk, or demeanor. He is unassuming to the degree and reluctantly speaks of his achievements. Laysan Island, which is the larger of the three, and the one from which the group derives its name, is now nearly worked out, all the work of extracting guano having been confined to it. In the near future one of the other islands will be worked and they will last a great many years as neither one of them has yet to be touched.

After his triumphant tour of the Pacific Northwest, Max returned aboard the *C. Kennedy* to Laysan Island, where he was prepared to conduct some serious business. He wished to further confirm his legal title to Laysan and Lisianski Islands. Presently, his only lease was the one which Pacific Guano and Fertilizer Company had had with the Hawaiian Government. This had been passed along to Max at the time of his purchase of the guano mining operation from P.G. and F. Co.

In March 1904, Max wrote to the Hawaiian Land Commissioner with a lease proposal. As time went on, Max received no response from the Land Commissioner. Later that year he wrote a letter to Hawaii's Governor Carter in which he again proposed that he be granted a 99-year lease for the islands of Laysan, Lisianski, and the French Frigate Shoals.

For this expansion of his "empire" he promised to plant 1,000 coconut trees each year and to pay 55 cents per ton of guano taken. He would protect the birds but wanted the privilege of killing the numbers of birds as per an attached list he sent along with the letter. He proposed that the skins be turned over to the Territorial Government to sell; they would retain 10 percent of the proceeds. He would maintain his residence on Laysan Island, keeping someone there to aid shipwrecked sailors when it was necessary for him to be away. He further proposed to maintain a schooner of not less than fifty gross tons register, which would be of service to the Territory to bring shipwrecked people to Honolulu at a reasonable price to be agreed upon.

It was also proposed that no rent would be paid for the first ten years; for the balance of the lease he would pay fifty dollars per annum in advance. He would employ laborers with families if possible, giving preference to Polynesians.

Included with his letter to Governor Carter was the following list of birds that Max proposed to kill each season as recorded in Smithsonian's Atoll Research Bulletin 171:

Variety	*NUMBER*
1. Black Widacks (Wideawakes=Sooty Terns)	5,000
2. Blue Widacks (Gray-backed Terns)	2,000
3. Large Black Birds (Brown Noddies)	200
4. Small Black Birds (Black Noddies)	200
5. Tropical Birds (Red-tailed Tropicbirds)	200
6. Love Birds (White Terns)	none
7. Four large kinds Mutton Birds (Bonin Petrels, Christmas Shearwaters, Wedge-tailed Shearwater)	5,000
8. Two small kinds of Mutton Birds(Sooty Storm Petrels and Bulwer's Petrels)	500
9. White Albatross (Laysan Albatross)	5,000
10. Black Gunies (Black-footed Albatross)	1,000
11. Frigate Birds (Great Frigatebirds)	All there could be killed
12. Large Bubbies (Blue-faced Boobies)	100
13. Small Bubbies (Red-footed Boobies)	100
14. Wingless Birds (Laysan Rails)	1,000
15. Canary Birds (Laysan Finches)	1,000
16. Red Birds (Laysan Honeyeaters)	100
17. Miller Birds or insect killer(Laysan Miller-birds)	100

Should the aforementioned proposition not be possible, he suggested submitting it to the President of the United States to secure a special Act of Congress to confirm his rights. As references, Max gave the names of H. Hackfeld and Co., F. A. Schafer and Co. and C.L. Wight.

He sent accompanying documents, six letters from Commander Thomas of the Albatross, mainly of a personal nature, but indicating that Mr. Schlemmer had rendered good service to the vessel and the personnel in their work.

The Governor's reply to Max Schlemmer was as follows:

Dec. 23, 1904

Captain Max Schlemmer

c/o Hackfeld and Co., Honolulu

Dear Sir,

Herewith, I return the letters received from you on Dec. 19th.

I have submitted the question as to whether or not it is possible and proper to give you some sort of police authority to prevent poaching on the leeward islands, to the High Sheriff.

If this is done, you can readily understand that you will be responsible to the Territorial Government and under its control and direction, so far as the exercise of your authority is concerned.

In reference to your proposition to lease the right to take a reasonable number of birds from Lisianski Island and the French Frigate Shoals, you introduce a new element by offering to plant no less than 1,000 coconut trees each year for ten years. And further, that you desire the privilege of taking guano from all three islands, paying a royalty of fifty cents a ton.

I am at a loss to know how many birds it would probably be safe to kill without affecting their numbers. I gathered from our conversation that you thought about ten thousand a season. Your proposition involves 21,800, exclusive of the French Frigate Shoals birds, which I assume are birds of prey.

One suggestion you make it seems to me not at all practicable—that the Territorial Government go into the question of the sale of birds. The policy of the Territorial should be, I believe, to keep out of business.

Naturally, I should refer the whole proposition to Mr. Pratt, the Commissioner of Public Lands, and when it is in shape, I would like to forward it to the Interior Department in Washington for its approval.

Very sincerely yours,

George R. Carter
Governor

Max never received confirmation that his lease proposal was accepted or approved. Not to be deterred, Max went ahead with his plans anyway.

8

HOLOCAUST AT SEA

By January 1905, the Schlemmer family had moved to Honolulu. During their early years, the family had stayed on Laysan Island the year round. But as the children got older and needed to be in school, the Schlemmer family usually took up residence in Honolulu during the off season winter months.

Max was in Honolulu harbor with his schooner, the *C.Kennedy*. He was taking supplies aboard for the cable company personnel and the U.S. Marine garrison. His plan was to stop at Laysan for a day or two, to attend to some business then go on to Midway Island with the supplies for the cable company and the marines there.

His departure was delayed for a time, awaiting the birth of their fifth child. On January 21, 1905, Therese gave birth to a daughter Regina Diana. On February 9th Captain Schlemmer was at the helm of his schooner on the high seas heading for Laysan Island. It would be the last voyage of the *C. Kennedy*.

On March 28, 1905, headlines of *The Hawaiian Star* read: "THE KING OF LAYSAN WRECKED." The paper carried a full account of the disaster on its front page.

According to the story, the ship encountered rough weather two days out, just after clearing the main islands. The *Kennedy* arrived at Laysan March 2nd, after 21 days out. She was tied up to a buoy on the west side of the island about a mile from the reef. Max completed his business ashore.

The following day, March 3rd Max weighed anchor for Midway. Under full sail, the *Kennedy* was cut loose from the buoy and was headed out to sea when suddenly a tempestuous wind and boiling surf came piling in from as far out as the eye could see. The small craft was helpless in the teeth of the storm. A riptide set in from the west. The combination of forces swept the schooner with irresistible force, stern first onto the reef.

She was a staunch little vessel and withstood the first shock and subsequent pounding for some time, but the *Kennedy* slowly broke apart. The lifeboats were launched and Captain Max and the crew started for shore, about 600 yards away. One of the boats capsized before reaching shore. The seas continued to pound at them, making their landing on shore quite perilous.

The storm had struck at 2:30 in the afternoon. Had it occurred at night, not a man would have reached shore alive. Fortunately, a few Japanese laborers had remained on Laysan to prepare a shipment of guano for the *Kennedy* on its return from Midway. Max and his companions were housed and fed. When the weather subsided, the work of trying to save as many of the stores as possible from the vessel began.

The mail for Midway was taken ashore. A considerable amount of the Naval and cable company's stores destined for Midway was also taken ashore. Much of the cargo was damaged. The ship was not insured. Max lost everything as did his mate J.C. Green who had purchased an interest in the venture. Both small boats were lost.

For Max, the contrast of his plight with the possibilities of a profitable cruise was heartbreaking. Twelve hundred tons of guano sat in the warehouse at Laysan. Another 500 tons sat in the field waiting to be collected. There was more than enough guano on Laysan to keep the little schooner running to Honolulu for months.

On March 17th, while Max and the crew moped about trying to cope with a bad situation, the gunboat *Petrel* came into sight and passed within two miles of Laysan. All ashore were certain the *Petrel* would stop and pick them up, but it steamed on past and went on to Midway. The ship's crew saw nothing of the wrecked craft and they had no reason to stop at Laysan. Besides there was a strong swell running at the time and it would not have been safe for the vessel to land.

The *Petrel* arrived at Midway March 19th, starting to unload its cargo at once even though it was Sunday. They had to lay off shore on Monday due to a heavy swell, but resumed work on Tuesday.

They sailed for Laysan the same day. The vessel arrived at Laysan to pick up a cargo of guano, March 28th and found the wrecked crew. That same evening, *The Hawawiian Star* newspaper hit the streets with the headlines; "The King of Laysan Wrecked"

Captain Max Schlemmer, J.C. Green, a second Mate Charles Krohn and six Japanese from the shipwrecked crew were taken aboard and the *Petrel* set sail for Honolulu. Max was united with his wife Therese and their five children. Whenever Max was at sea, Therese was especially worried. She knew that Max couldn't swim.

It was now April and the beginning of the guano mining season on Laysan Island. With the loss of the *Kennedy*, the King of Laysan was now in desperate need of a ship that would take him and his family back to Laysan Island. Shortly thereafter he was able to charter the schooner *Levi Woodbury*.

Before he left for Laysan, Max received a letter from the Commander of the *U.S.S. Iroquois*, a Navy tug. The Commander offered to tow the *Levi Woodbury*, with the Schlemmer family aboard, to Laysan by way of Midway.

The family and the schooner, *Levi Woodbury*, would be left at Laysan after the run to Midway. The Commander of the *Iroquois* needed extra cargo space to store supplies bound for Midway. Captain Harris of the *Woodbury* agreed. The seagoing tug, *Iroquois*, with the *Woodbury* in tow set off with the Schlemmer family tucked safely below.

The waters off the Kauai coast were extremely rough that evening. The cargo on the deck of the *Woodbury* was piled up even with the ship's rail. The supercargo, a fellow in charge of the freight, was named Clark. He came out of the cabin and sat atop the cargo. An enormous swell lifted the tug so it towered over the little schooner. It came crashing down with a solid thud. The *Woodbury* shuddered from bow to stern. Clark was thrown overboard by the force of the collision and was never seen again.

The *Woodbury* weathered the storm and the Schlemmer family arrived safely at their home on Laysan Island. There the schooner took aboard 90 tons of guano and sailed for Honolulu.

Meanwhile though, as the Schlemmer family was ensconced at home on Laysan Island, the Honolulu newspapers were chronicling a story of yet another Max

Schlemmer disaster. Captain William Weisbarth, skipper of the schooner, *Lavinia*, was reporting the possibility that the *Woodbury* with Max aboard, had been lost at sea.

In mid July, about the time the *Woodbury* left Laysan bound for Honolulu, there was a terrible 3-day storm in the area. Captain Weisbarth with his schooner *Lavinia* was also caught in the storm. It took Weisbarth 27 days to make port in Honolulu and the little schooner was badly damaged.

One of the Honolulu papers reported that *Levi Woodbury* and her master, Max Schlemmer were lost and Captain Weisbarth, aboard his schooner *Lavinia*, set sail to search for the *Levi Woodbury*.

> At 1:45 yesterday morning, the schooner *Lavinia*, with Schlemmer's old companion in arms, Weisbarth in command, left the harbor and started for Laysan.
>
> If Schlemmer is to be found, Weisbarth believes he can do the job. Schlemmer and Weisbarth are like Damon and Pythias, when they are not squabbling over little matters of navigation, but, when danger besets one, the other is willing to sacrifice his all to rescue him.

In early August, the *Woodbury* docked in Honolulu, a bit overdue with some damage but otherwise intact. The Schlemmer family remained at Laysan, never in real danger.

Things were quiet on Laysan in 1906, except for the birth of their sixth child, Otto Paul Conrad Schlemmer. He was born Sept. 30, 1906. Otto was not to play a significant role in his Father's life. It was his older brother Eric who was to become "The Prince of Laysan."

As Otto grew older, he and Max never saw eye to eye on much of anything. Max thought Otto was incorrigible. As a last resort, he sent Otto to the Coast Guard station in Honolulu. He strongly suggested to the Commander that they enlist Otto. Perhaps they could make something out of him. Otto found his niche in the Coast Guard. Shortly after World War II, he returned to Honolulu. He was the first person born in Hawaii to command a Coast Guard ship in Hawaiian waters.

9

INTRIGUE IN HIGH PLACES

In May 1907, Max was low on supplies. He waited anxiously at Laysan for the arrival of either the *Iwalani* or the schooner *Lavinia*, which often called at Laysan to pick up a cargo of guano. Although Max bore a grudge toward Weisbarth, the skipper of the *Lavinia*, he still had a great deal of admiration for Weisbarth's skill and seamanship.

To Max's surprise, however, the *Annapolis* arrived, skippered by Captain Clark. The ship had both mail and supplies for them. When Max inquired about the *Iwalani* and the *Lavinia*, the Captain told him the *Iwalani* was not coming and the *Lavinia* had been shipwrecked.

Max made inquiries about the possibility of passage on the *Annapolis*, bound for Honolulu, for himself and his daughters, Mary and Ottilie. The most pressing matter for Max was to tend to the business of chartering a ship to haul guano to Honolulu. Mary and Ottilie needed to attend school in Honolulu. While there he would settle the girls with family. He was able to secure passage on the *Annapolis* for himself and two young daughters Mary and Ottilie, and they departed for Honolulu May 18, 1907.

On the *Annapolis*, they were treated like royalty. It was a memorable trip for all. My Mother, Ottilie, the first born on Laysan, was registered to attend school at St. Andrews Priory in Honolulu. The letter she wrote from Honolulu to her mother on Laysan Island is evidence, however that she had learned well from home schooling and from sketchy formal schooling.

When Max arrived in Honolulu, he had with him a letter giving him power of attorney to draw money from his wife's bank account. With this money he was to buy or charter a schooner in her name. After several unsuccessful attempts to charter a ship, one day Max wandered into downtown Honolulu where he ran into an old acquaintance, Alex Dowsett, outside the Union Grill on King Street. Alex had a small fleet of schooners.

Kalihi Honolulu,
May 15th 1907.

Dear Mamma;
          We arrived here safe and
well but Mary and I were sea-sick. We are
all well and hope you are well to. We are eating
lots of papais and bananas and are getting
whiter Gussie is fat and a little biger then
Mary. We have been visiting lots of people.
On the steamer we had ice-cream and we were
offered on silver-trays we ate with silver spoons
we all call our-selves the three Princess nd
papa the king. We enjoy our-selves quite much
here are no mangoes so we can-not send
any we have eaten lots of candies and
are just sweet. Kiss the little ones for me. Mildred
and Cathrine are glad that they have a
little sister two weeks old. I play with Mildre
-d and Cathrine and my other friends.
Here I see no Gunies but sparrows have
little nests with eggs. Here are lots of maquit-
-es here Antie Julia has more moquitoes then
we have. Papa will tell you all the news with
lots of loves and kisses.   I remain
       your loving Daughter.
          Ottilie Schlemmer.

Ottilie's letter from Honolulu to her mother on Laysan Island.

However, Alex had no schooner available to be chartered, all were needed for
his own use. During their conversation, they discussed the bad luck Max had

encountered over the past two years. Then Max launched into a tirade against the Territorial Government that allowed Japanese pirates to make thousands of dollars stealing birds at Laysan and especially at Lisianski Island, both U.S. possessions.

He complained that this was occurring even while Governor Carter had on his desk a letter from Max Schlemmer proposing to pay the government a percentage for the privilege of slaughtering a certain number of birds a year. Alex Dowsett was now giving Max some serious attention.

He asked what Max would give the government. Max replied, "For every ten, one." Max meant for every ten birds he killed for plumage, he would give the government one. The King of Laysan was warming up to his favorite subject, the vast amount of money that could be made from bird skins.

Suddenly, their conversation was rudely interrupted by Arthur Brown, the ex High Sheriff of Honolulu. Brown had overheard the conversation. He loudly announced that Max was "Just the fellow I've been looking for." Max excused himself from Dowsett and was spirited away down the street by his new acquaintance.

In his journal account, Max tells the following story. He calls it, "intrigue in high places." At dinner in Brown's Waikiki home the following evening, Brown explained to Max that A.L.C. Atkinson, the acting governor was his brother-in-law. He told Max that the two of them had discussed at some length the profit that could be made in the bird business. Max was questioned late into the night regarding all aspects of the trade in bird parts and skins. They agreed to meet the following morning at Brown's office.

When Max arrived the next day, the ex-sheriff got right to the point. Brown told Max that while indeed there was a fortune to be made, Max was going around town talking too much. Max agreed. He was glad he had finally found a friend, knowledgeable about the potential bird business and with whom he could discuss plans.

Brown told Max that Governor Carter was going to be away and that Atkinson was to be the acting Governor. Brown also felt that Atkinson would soon be appointed Governor to succeed Carter. He went on to say that Atkinson, Gilman, Pratt and himself were interested in forming a company to engage in the bird trade with Schlemmer as manager and shareholder.

The first order of business, Brown further explained, would be for Atkinson to obtain a long-term lease for Laysan as the present lease had been cancelled. Max was furious. He asked who had cancelled the lease. Brown told him Hackfeld had cancelled it. Max told Brown that he had the lease for Laysan. He had been told that it had expired, but now Max was hearing for the first time that the lease had been cancelled. Brown suggested to Max that if he had lease papers, they would go after Hackfeld to have the lease reinstated.

But the lease documents were on Laysan Island. Max decided to leave at once to go to Laysan to get them. But before this scheme became too involved, Brown wanted Max to understand that the names of Atkinson and Pratt should be kept quiet. It would not look good for the Governor and the Land Commissioner to be involved in such an enterprise.

Before leaving for Laysan to retrieve the lease documents, Max must attend to the business for which he had come to Honolulu. A schooner had to be purchased, for his own use as well as his potential business partnership. Max had inspected the *Luka* and thought she was what they needed. Brown wanted a second opinion. He got it from Lyle Alex. Alex claimed it was a bargain for $2,500.00 or $3,000.00.

Max drew the money from Therese's account and made a down payment for the purchase of the *Luka*, in his wife's name. The balance of the agreement of sale was to be paid the following day by his partners.

When Max arrived at Arthur Brown's office the next day, he was told that Mr. Brown was sick. Max left the office and headed up Fort Street where he was stopped by a friend of Brown's, a Mr. Gillman. Gillman told Max that Brown did not want him to buy the ship. If Max went ahead with the purchase, he would have to take the responsibility for payment in full.

When Max finally caught up with Brown at his office, Brown denied having agreed to the purchase of a ship. After a long and heated discussion it was agreed that Max would pay the balance owed on the *Luka*. Brown would then pay all the expenses to outfit the ship, purchase supplies and hire a crew with power of attorney from Max Schlemmer. With that understanding they formed a partnership. Max was now prepared to leave for Laysan Island.

Max sailed to Laysan with three men aboard the *Luka*. His mission was to send the lease document back to Brown together with a sample collection of bird skins. At Laysan, they loaded the *Luka* with guano and sent her back to Honolulu with the lease documents, and bird skin samples.

By late summer 1907, Max realized he must get to Honolulu and find out what was happening with the partnership he had formed with Arthur Brown and A.L.C. Atkinson. Meanwhile, he had learned that Atkinson had not been appointed Governor; Frear was Governor.

When he reached Honolulu, Max's first order of business was to visit Atkinson at his office. Atkinson's enthusiasm remained high about the prospects of a lucrative business. He had gotten word recently, through the Japanese, about the enormous sum of money to be made on these northwestern bird islands.

In one season, a Japanese schooner Captain wrote that, he "took 157,000 skins that amounted to $65,000.00."

Atkinson told Brown and Max that they had to get control of Laysan and Lisianski Islands at any cost. Max's lease had expired and would not suffice for their purpose. Atkinson went on to say that they would try for a lease from the Territorial Government, but failing this, they would try to purchase the islands outright.

Atkinson had property in Honolulu that could be exchanged and a wealthy Colonel friend with money to back him up. Big plans were swirling about him but Max began to feel that the scheme was slipping away from him and into the hands of those in "high places." He quietly departed and decided that if anything were to come of such a venture, he would probably have to make his own deal.

10

THE SAGA OF THE LUKA

Meantime, in early summer 1907, when Max arrived back on Laysan aboard the *Luka*, he made haste to collect the bird skin samples and the lease documents. He loaded the guano cargo, so that the *Luka* could set sail for Honolulu as soon as possible.

Max also included a letter to be hand delivered to Arthur Brown. In this letter he asked Brown to discharge the skipper he had hired to take the *Luka* to Honolulu. Max didn't trust him. Max suggested to Brown that he hire Captain Harris or as a last resort, Captain William Weisbarth.

At Laysan, Max waited anxiously for the return of the *Luka*. A month went by. Max was certain the trip should have taken much less time. On July 1st, they spotted a schooner. They were sure it was the *Luka*. But as it came closer, they could see that it was much larger and also flying a Japanese flag.

Once the schooner dropped anchor, Max armed himself with a .38 caliber Smith and Wesson pistol and prepared to board the ship. With him were Paul Bomke, Therese's brother, who had recently come to work on the island, and two Japanese workers. The workers stayed in the boat alongside the Japanese ship. If there was trouble they were to go ashore. Therese would have rifles for them to stop the intruders.

The Captain proved to be friendly. He told Max he was short on provisions and water. Max told him he could have all the water he wanted, but no provisions. The Captain asked Max to keep four of his men and take them to Honolulu. Max agreed. If they would work, Max would pay them. The four Japanese brought their belongings ashore on July 2nd. The Japanese ship departed the next day bound for Johnson Island. Max took the four men ashore with him.

Max soon learned the men left behind by the "nice" Japanese skipper were nothing but a bunch of scoundrels. They wouldn't work and constantly caused trouble. All four of them were often drunk and disorderly. The trouble got serious when Therese suddenly became ill.

The Schlemmer's cook with vodka bottles confiscated from the workers' quarters of the four Japanese left on Laysan by the Japanese schooner

While she was sick, Paul Bomke found, by accident, a recently buried jar containing a deadly poison. She recovered but Max was sure his wife had been poisoned. He called the men together and questioned them. Two of the more surly individuals said the Captain had given them the poison. The other two were young kids who knew little of what was going on. Max began to wonder about the possibility of a deadly plot to kill the family and take control of the island. The Captain of the Japanese ship just might have been on a bird pirating expedition.

Max told the four Japanese castaways that he no longer had work for them and that he would not pay them. Furthermore, when they got to Honolulu he would have them arrested. Later, the Schlemmer's Japanese cook came to Max and said he agreed that the men were troublemakers and should not be paid. But he pleaded with Max not to have them arrested. Max agreed, but he couldn't help but be suspicious of the men and continued to believe they were involved in a plot to poison the Schlemmer family.

After the Japanese ship left Laysan, everyone continued to keep a sharp lookout for the *Luka*. She was several weeks overdue.

Finally, it was the *Iroquois* that arrived. Captain Carter asked Max when the *Luka* had left Laysan for Honolulu. Max told him the ship had never arrived at Laysan. The Captain could not believe this. The *Luka* had been out for 41 days.

Max also learned that neither Captain Harris nor Weisbarth had command of the *Luka*. It was Captain Olsen. In the meantime the *Luka* returned to Honolulu. It had been out 45 days and had been unable to find Laysan Island. Captain Olsen became the laughing stock of Honolulu when he declared that Laysan had been destroyed by a seismic disturbance.

After the *Luka* fiasco, Arthur Brown realized that the *Luka* must return to Laysan but this time it would have to be skippered by one of the men that Max had recommended. And so it was Captain William Weisbarth who boarded the *Luka* and set sail for Laysan. The *Luka* arrived without incident, in 10 days.

Now Max set out to prove to the world that his Kingdom on Laysan had not sunk below the waves. A news article dated September 19, 1907, reported that "the *Luka*, under the command of Captain Max Schlemmer, had arrived in Honolulu early the previous morning after a run of 18 days from Laysan Island. She had light winds and calm waters all the way. About 85 tons of guano were brought back in the hold and on deck."

There were several other news articles regarding the *Luka*'s "freight of canary birds, shark fins, sucker fish, pilot fish, dolphins and red paint." A coat of red paint gave her a festive air. The little vessel presented a gala appearance as she entered the harbor. Her flag was flying high as if to say, "We found Laysan Island this time. She's still in the same place she always was."

The Schooner *Luka*. Photo from collection of J. J. Williams, Bishop Museum

Although Max proved that Laysan Island did not sink, the *Luka* turned out to be an economic disaster. On November 14th, 1907, the Japanese crew filed suit against the *Luka* for lost wages.

Four days later, Arthur Brown filed suit against the ship's owner, Therese Schlemmer. Brown claimed he had spent $507.64 and pledged another $834.87 for stores, provisions and labor to outfit the *Luka*. Brown had spent this money at the time the ship was first purchased for a business partnership that never materialized. Brown further claimed that he had done all this in good faith as the ship's agent. Brown asked for another $250.00 for his services.

The schooner was sold at auction to Arthur Brown for $1,000.00. When Brown was unable to pay the balance, the *Luka* was again auctioned. This time it went for $400.00 to C. Mincke, a Kauai rancher.

11

THE DEPARTURE OF CAPTAIN WEISBARTH

The year 1907 had not been a good year for Max Schlemmer. He was sad and depressed when he watched the *Luka*'s sails disappear over the horizon as she made her way to her new home on the island of Hawaii. Nevertheless his spirits were somewhat raised when he heard the news that his old nemesis, Captain William Weisbarth was about to leave Hawaii for good.

Captain William Weisbarth and family at Laysan Island.

The old sea dog's luck had run out. His schooner had been wrecked in a storm and he had barely escaped with his life. The following newspaper article tells about his departure:

> Bound for the Gilbert Islands, almost 2500 miles away, in the little twenty eight foot ketch *Keoki*, Capt. William Weisbarth, will depart today on an ocean voyage that has attracted much attention in shipping circles here.
>
> Mrs. Weisbarth, the captain's wife, will accompany her husband on this long and adventurous voyage, and is looking forward with pleasure to the hour of sailing. In addition to these two venturesome spirits, the vessel will carry a crew of three. The *Keoki* is well stocked with water, provisions and household effects. The latter will be used by the Weisbarth's in establishing their new home in the South Seas. They plan to stop at Palmyra Island for a fresh supply of water.
>
> Captain Weisbarth expressed no fear yesterday as to the outcome of the trip. He said at this time of the year the wind and weather conditions were most favorable for a quick and smooth passage to the Gilberts. It is estimated that the trip will take at least sixty days. Mrs. Weisbarth was born in the Gilbert Islands and is said to hold extensive landholdings there. Captain Weisbarth is no stranger in those waters, having spent many years as a trader there before coming to Hawaii.
>
> Captain Weisbarth and his wife intend to spend the remainder of their lives in the Gilberts. Many of the couple's friends will be at pier No. 10 today to see them off and wish them bon voyage on their long and venturesome trip.

This newspaper article was accompanied by "A Toast to Captain Weisbarth" a poem written by an "old shipmate," Max Schlemmer.

> Weisbarth, you old sea dog,
> Spawn of the salt sea foam,
> Here's wishing a smile
> For each watery mile,
> When your craft bears you home.
>
> Weisbarth, you old German,
> Son of a Saxon bold.
> May the southern seas,
> With their balmy breeze,
> Abundance of wealth unfold.

Weisbarth, my old shipmate,
Of all the very best,
Here's hoping that you
And your valiant crew,
Will find a haven of rest.

Once Weisbarth was gone, Max's euphoria somewhat subsided. However, in May 1907, Max received a Police Constable's commission, something he had sought for many months. The official document stated that his authority was "within the county of Oahu and more particularly for and within Honolulu and the Western Group."

When the commission was granted, Governor Carter made it very clear that the authority herein was primarily for the protection of the birds and to prevent poaching. Although it was a position without pay, the fact that he had police authority over Laysan and Lisianski Islands was all that Max wanted for now.

Ever the entrepreneur, the dauntless Max soon unveiled his next venture. An article in the *Evening Bulletin*, April 23, 1908 in Honolulu announced that "the well-known King of Laysan was about to establish a tannery on Laysan Island."

The name of the company was to be Heine and Co. Mr. Heine was one of the most expert tanners in the business, having learned the trade years ago in Stockton, California. Details of the business were sketchy.

The tanning business may seem somewhat incongruous with Max's other ventures. But it should be noted that sometime between the years 1902 and 1903, Max brought "a slew of rabbits" to Laysan Island. His intention was that the rabbits would supply fresh meat for the family and pets for the children. Now with the proposed tannery, the question may have been asked, Was the tannery for the purpose of processing rabbit hides or bird skins? We'll never know. Nothing more was ever heard about this project. Much more however, is heard about the rabbits. As is typical, they multiplied rapidly, and were soon munching their way into what was to become one of Hawaii's greatest ecological disasters.

12

A DEAL WITH THE DEVIL

By mid 1908, Max was feeling frustrated, and perhaps somewhat desperate. He was also in poor financial straits. While the guano mining business was dwindling, nothing else seemed to be working out. His hopes for making the great sums of money promised by getting into the bird plumage business, had been dashed. He had been abandoned by his friends in "high places".

Now he set out, as he put it, to make a "deal with the devil." He decided to go to Japan on a business trip. His departure was delayed however, when Therese gave birth to their seventh child. Eva Schlemmer was born in Honolulu on November 5, 1908.

On December 22, 1908, Max negotiated a contract in Tokyo with Genkichi Yamanouchi. Max was to receive $150.00 a month in gold in Honolulu. For this monthly stipend, the Japanese were given rights inherent in his agent's commission to remove and sell "phosphate, guano, and products of whatever nature in and from the islands of Laysan and Lisianski."

The contract was to run for 15 years. Schlemmer promised to prevent others from infringing on the Japanese privileges by use of his police authority.

About six weeks after this contract was concluded, on February 8, 1909, Schlemmer finally received a lease from the Territorial Government for Laysan and Lisianski. It stipulated that the government might reclaim the lands at any time for public purposes. Max was directed to plant 500 coconut trees per year. He was not to use explosives to capture fish, nor allow the destruction or capture of birds. He was to pay fifty cents per ton of guano removed. This lease was for fifteen years at an annual rental of $25.31.

Meanwhile, President Theodore Roosevelt issued executive order 1019 on February 3, 1909, declaring the Hawaiian archipelago to be the Hawaiian Islands Bird Reservation. It placed the following under the jurisdiction of the U.S. Dept. of Agriculture: Cure Island, Pearl and Hermes Reef, Lisianski or Pell Island, Maro Reef, Laysan Island, Dowsett Reef, Gardiner Island, Two Brothers Reef,

French Frigate Shoal, Necker Island, Frost Shoal, and Big Bird Island. (All names and spellings from original documents.)

On June, 1909, the Commandant of the naval station in Hawaii was authorized by the Secretary of Navy to put the Executive Order into effect. Naval forces at his command, together with other forces he could requisition, were to be used, if necessary, for maintenance of laws governing the preservation of birds and their breeding grounds on the Hawaiian Islands Bird Reservation.

Late in 1909, rumors surfaced in Honolulu that bird pirates were once again raiding the Northwestern Hawaiian Islands. The U.S. Revenue Cutter *Thetis* under the command of W.V.E. Jacobs was sent to investigate. The *Thetis* arrived at Laysan in the late afternoon on January 16, 1910. An armed crew was sent ashore where they found fifteen Japanese workmen using thirteen deserted buildings which had been erected, by the Pacific Guano and Fertilizer Co.

Captain Jacobs made the following report:

> One building was full of the breast feathers of birds in bulk, another was two-thirds full of loose bird wings and two other buildings were partly filled with bales of feathers and wings, and a number of stuffed birds. On the sand adjacent to the buildings were about two hundred mats held down with rocks, under which were laid out masses of birds' wings in various stages of curing. Stretched along the beach and over the island were bodies of dead birds in large numbers from which emanated obnoxious odors.

The following day, a crew was again sent ashore. They arrested the Japanese, seized the plumage and loaded it aboard the *Thetis*. Operations were completed by the 18th. All told, sixty-five bales of bird wings, twenty-eight large and three small bags of feathers, thirteen bales of feathers and two boxes of stuffed birds were confiscated. This amounted to about a ton of feathers and an estimated 119,000 bird wings.

Further investigation by Jacobs revealed that a raid led by Masayeshi Houme on April 17, prior to the arrival of the *Thetis*, netted a ton of feathers and 128,000 wings. About August 10th, a portion of feathers and wings were taken aboard the *Tempou Maru* and shipped to Japan.

From April 13, 1909 through January 16, 1910 the Japanese had two work parties; one on Laysan and one on Lisianski. During that period, two and a quarter tons of feathers and 310,000 bird wings were gathered. The lowest price these materials brought was $.33 per wing and $6.00 a pound for feathers. The materials gathered at Laysan would have been worth about $131,000.

The Japanese overseer claimed they had a right to be on the island. As evidence he presented his documents to Commander Jacobs. These documents were seized by Jacobs. They included the agent's commission to Max Schlemmer from the Pacific Guano and Fertilizer Co., and the contract agreement between Schlemmer and Genkichi Yamanouchi concerning Yamanouchi's rights on the islands of Laysan and Lisianski. Another contract seized was between Schlemmer and Yamanouchi by which Max recognized the capture of birds by Yamanouchi. The documents taken also included Schlemmer's Police Constable's Commission.

13

THE KING DEPOSED

On November 30, 1909, Max received the following letter from E. A. Mott Smith, Acting Governor, Territory of Hawaii:

Dear Sir:

I have to inform you that we have received advices from the Secretary of the Interior that the Commissioner of Public Lands of the Territory was on February 8, 1909, without jurisdiction or authority to execute the lease to you of the islands of Laysan and Lisianski, an executive order having been made by the President of the United States on February 3, 1909, which appropriated these islands to the use and purposes of the federal government. It has been held by the Secretary of Interior that such appropriation terminated territorial control; at least to the extent that the Territory was without authority to execute said lease to you.

You are therefore requested to return your copy of the lease, in order that cancellation thereof may be duly entered upon our records.

Very respectfully,

E.A. Mott Smith
Acting Governor

Max had become aware of the President's declaring that the islands of Laysan and Lisianski were included in the Hawaiian Islands Reservation. His executive order, dated February 3, 1909, "hereby reserved and set apart, (these islands) subject to valid existing rights, for the use of the Department of Agriculture as a preserve and breeding ground for native birds." As early as July, Max began writing to the Governor for a clarification of his lease. There was no response. Finally in a letter dated October 6, 1909, to Governor Walter F. Frear, Max wrote:

I'd be willing to cancel my lease of Laysan and Lisianski Islands for the sum of Two Thousand Dollars ($2000), including everything as it stands and four thousand coconut trees, which are newly planted.

In an immediate response to this letter, Governor Frear wrote to Max October 7, 1909:

The Territory of course cannot pay you for a cancellation of the lease; indeed, it is immaterial to the Territory whether the lease is cancelled or not. What view the authorities in Washington take as to the validity of the lease they have not yet indicated.

The letter of November 30, 1909 to Max from Acting Governor Mott Smith would seem to state the "view the authorities in Washington take." Max received a letter from Governor Frear dated December 4, 1911:

I have your letter of the 3rd instant; am sorry to learn that you have had so much trouble and so many difficulties. We, of course, could not avoid your losing the lease of Lisianski Island. I hope things will go better for you in the future.

By early November, 1909, news about Max's loss of his lease of the islands, had reached Honolulu. On November 11, 1909, headlines from the *Honolulu Advertiser* proclaimed: "King Max of Laysan is Deposed." The article went on to say:

Max Schlemmer is no longer the King of Laysan. He has been deposed; his Kingdom has been taken away from him. He is now a King without a throne, a monarch exiled from his land.

There has been no revolt among the subjects of King Max. His rule has been mild and beneficent and his people have always been well satisfied. It is only a case of a stronger power stepping in and taking away his land. The U.S. government is the power that has deposed the King of Laysan and annexed his country.

On November 10th, the *Advertiser* had received the following cablegram from its special correspondent in Washington:

Ballinger has cancelled Max Schlemmer's guano lease, holding that the Territory had no authority to lease the Island of Laysan.

A follow up article sounded a nostalgic note:

> King Max has lost his throne and his kingdom, the little sand spit lying lonely in the midst of the Pacific which has been his home and the home of his family, the windswept isle where he has brought up his children. The place where he made so many long voyages to and from, is no more. One more of the Kings of the Pacific has been deposed.

While U.S. District Attorney Brekens waited for advice from Washington, Max and his attorney, Arthur Milder, hatched a plot they thought would help Max avoid prosecution. They offered to pay rent to the Territorial Government for Laysan and Lisianski. The rationale was that if they were paying rent, how could they be prosecuted for using resources on these islands? Their offer was refused. A federal grand jury was formed. Schlemmer was charged with violation of the contract labor law. If he was found guilty he could be fined $1,000.00 for each laborer brought into the territory.

On March 22, 1910, Max Schlemmer, the former "King of Laysan" was indicted by the federal grand jury for importing contract laborers and for allowing poaching on a bird reservation. He was released on a $1,000.00 bond. The 23 Japanese who spent 24 hours in jail were being held as witnesses for the prosecution.

At the trial, Schlemmer's attorney contended that President Roosevelt had no authority to create the Hawaiian Islands Bird Reservation. Such authority lay with the U.S. Congress, he contended, which in this case was lacking. Prosecutor Breckons charged that the 23 Japanese arrested by the *Thetis* were illegally in the country and that they were brought in by Max Schlemmer.

Judge Robertson allowed the defense five days in which to file a memorandum of the cases cited in support of its contentions. He gave the prosecution five days in which to answer. Along with the suit against Max, one was filed against one of the Japanese. It was a test case, which, if successful, would have been the basis for action against other Japanese.

The case was unsuccessful. The Japanese got free passage home and Max Schlemmer was found not guilty. However, District Attorney Breckons appealed the judge's decision but dropped the charge of poaching. He reworded the charges slightly, and in June, Max was again indicted on two counts of bringing aliens into the country illegally.

The Judge ruled that, "It is no offense and it is not unlawful to bring aliens by vessel and land them within the United States of America through and by means of others." Max was again found not guilty.

At this time, Max sorely needed an income. He had a large family to support and his legal fees were mounting. In July, 1910, he became custodian of the Odd Fellows Hall in Honolulu.

On October 2, 1911 the Schlemmer's eighth child, a girl named Adele was born in Honolulu. (Seven years later Adele died of diphtheria.)

By 1912, the rabbits, which Max had brought to Laysan Island in the early 1900s, had become a serious problem there. On the recommendation of William A. Bryan of the Bishop Museum in Honolulu, the U.S. Bureau of Biological Survey sent a party to exterminate the rabbits. They were also there to determine the condition of bird colonies, introduce coconuts, and transfer Laysan Rails from Laysan to Lisianski.

The party consisted of Commodore G.R. Salisbury (USN) William Wallace from Stanford University, George Willett from the Bureau of Biological Survey, and Alfred M. Bailey from the Denver Museum of Natural History. D.T. Fullaway of Honolulu accompanied the party to collect insects. They arrived at Laysan on December 21st. The Biological Survey party remained on Laysan until March 11, 1913. They killed 5,024 rabbits, but were not able to exterminate them all.

14

A SAD RETURN TO LAYSAN

By the winter of 1908, the Max Schlemmer family appeared to be permanently settled in Honolulu. They lived on Gulick Ave. in Kalihi Valley. However, Max continued to dream and scheme about returning to Laysan Island to make his home there.

Once again, the first order of business was to purchase a schooner. Through friends, Max heard about "the sloop yacht *Helene* lying at Pearl Harbor," owned by George Tait. The purchase price was $400.00 and the assumption by the buyer of the debts against the *Helene* not to exceed $275.00 as per the creditors bills filed against the sloop.

Somehow, Max scraped together the $400.00. The sale was notarized in the City and County of Honolulu, Territory of Hawaii, on August 4, 1914. Shortly thereafter, a newspaper article announced that Max would sail shortly to his former home on Laysan Island where he would establish a pearl fishery. Financial backing was in the works, but failed to materialize. Max evidently then dropped altogether his plans for the fishery.

By 1915, the bird pirates had struck again in the Northwestern Hawaiian Islands. Beginning as early as 1910, the Coast Guard ship, the *U.S.S. Thetis*, had visited the Hawaiian Bird Reservation on scientific and surveying missions. They were also to observe and report conditions as to the evidence of poaching and bird plundering. This latter mission was assigned by the Commandant of the navy forces in Hawaii. The Executive Order which had established the Hawaiian Islands Bird Reservation, gave the navy in Hawaii the task of protecting these bird islands from poachers and bird plunderers.

The *Thetis* had stopped on Laysan as often as twice a year. Now on April 3, 1915, the *Thetis* arrived on Laysan Island on a surveying mission. The Executive Officer, Lt. William H. Munter, led a shore party, which spent five hours surveying the island.

He reported that the island had been visited by the bird pirates. He estimated that between one hundred fifty and two hundred thousand birds were found lying in heaps. They lay on their backs with only their breast feathers removed. Most of the birds slaughtered were Laysan Albatross. The others were Black-footed Albatross (Gooney), Frigate birds, and blue-faced Booby. Also, a fair amount of decaying turtle meat and a few rabbits were strewn about. Lt. Munter was sickened by the sight of such depredation.

In May 1915, shortly after the *Thetis* arrived back in Honolulu, Lt. Munter went to see Max at Odd Fellows Hall. Munter had learned that Max wanted the job as Federal Warden for the islands of Laysan and Lisianski and had applied at one time, without success, for this job.

Munter introduced himself and told Max about his recent trip to Laysan on the *Thetis* and what he had found there. He went on to tell Max that he was impressed with what he had heard from people regarding Max personally. And certainly Munter was impressed as well, with Max's having lived on Laysan Island, and his knowledge of the birds there. Munter was most enthusiastic that Max was eminently qualified to be Federal Warden in this Northwestern Bird Reservation. Both he and Captain Brown, Skipper of the *Thetis*, were very unhappy with the conditions they found on Laysan Island. They were sincere in their desire to help secure the position of Federal Warden for Max Schlemmer.

Max was advised to get together all the recommendations he could. Munter would see that these recommendations reached the right persons in Washington. Max immediately set about gathering recommendations from Professor William A. Bryan, Mayor Lane, Governor Pinkham, retired Commander-in-Chief of the Pacific, Rear Admiral Chauncy Thomas, and Captain Niblack of the U.S. Navy.

Within a short time, these letters were given to Munter. About a week later, Munter again contacted Max. He suggested that Max try to get to Laysan as soon as he could. Munter explained to Max that Max being "on the job" might further enhance his chances that Washington would award the job of Federal Warden to him. Furthermore, the *Thetis* was out of order. Its machinery was being repaired and it would be two or three months before it could get underway. Max agreed that he should set sail for Laysan at the earliest possible date, but he felt obliged to give his employer a month's notice. He told Munter he would sail on June 25th. Captain Brown, commander of the *Thetis* relayed this information to Washington.

A month before Max set sail on the *Helene,* the war in Europe took a bad turn. The British ocean liner *Lusitania* was hit by German torpedoes and sunk. One hundred and twenty four American lives were lost.

People in America were beginning to take sides in the war and this incident only heightened suspicion of, and anger toward Germans. There were already those in Hawaii who viewed the Germans with jaundiced eyes. Max, now an American citizen was confident that he would be an exception to the anti-German sentiment sweeping the country.

The *Helene* left Honolulu harbor at 4:30 P.M. on June 25th, as Max promised. On board with Captain Max were his two sons Eric, twelve, and Otto, nine, and his daughter Mary, who was to do the cooking and make out all reports. Also along was Harold Brant, a twenty-one year Norwegian crewman who would join the workforce once they arrived on Laysan Island.

They sailed for Kauai amidst a squall and heavy rains. It was dark when they reached Kauai. They headed for the lighthouse and stood offshore until morning. At daybreak, the *Helene* passed Kilauea Lighthouse and dipped the flag when they saw a man waving to them.

As they passed Hanalei, Max dipped the flag to Mr. Birkmeyer and some of his old friends from the Inn. Passing Wainiha, Max again dipped the flag at sight of his friend, Mrs. George Titcomb who stood on shore with a gathering of other Kama'ainas.

After being becalmed off Mana Point, they finally picked up a light breeze and made for Waimea, but were unable to get in before dark. The *Helene* was now leaking badly. Some provisions were ruined, and most all of their clothes got wet.

Otto and Mary were quite seasick and didn't want to go any further. Max hailed a passing Sampan and put them aboard. They could stay with friends and relatives in Waimea, before getting home to Honolulu.

He tried to make it into the harbor that night, but it was very dark. Eric and Harold Brant were sent ahead in a small boat to make soundings. But as the *Helene* approached the entrance of the harbor, the lead line broke. Max was not about to take a chance. He dropped anchor outside the harbor to wait for morning.

The next morning, July 1st, the sky was cloudy and very high seas were running. Max had to make a dash for it. He left Waimea at five o'clock that morning. With a strong Northeast wind in her sails, the *Helene* headed for Laysan Island.

On the evening of July 12th, Eric spotted land. As a "sometime" Skipper, Max had not done a great deal of navigating. He thanked God that his chronometer and logline corresponded to his reckoning.

The following morning they went ashore. Max was stunned by what he saw. A scene of desolation, an empty desert lay before him. Just a few birds, no grass! He was sick. The houses and other buildings, which remained from the days of guano mining, were in a sad state of dilapidation. Windows and doors were missing; in some cases, parts of the roof and sides had caved in. Sand had drifted in and filled porches and rooms. Two coconut trees, which Max had planted in 1895, were about all that showed signs of survival though they were bent and stunted. Water storage tanks lay in ruins. It was a different place. Max was unable to speak. He was terribly glad that Mary and Otto were not with them. In a daze, the "King" walked about what was once his verdant, prosperous, thriving domain. What lay before him now was a desert strewn with bird carcasses. The sun beat down on them and created a terrible stench. More than a few rabbits remained; the only sign of life as they scampered about devouring what few sprouts dared emerge from the sandy waste.

The next morning Max hiked to the southern end of the island. In his journal he recorded the following:

> I discovered two turtles and a sleeping monk seal. Because we had no cooking oil or fresh meat, I shot the seal and flipped the turtles onto their backs. The boys pulled the turtles to a shack on lines fastened to their flippers. They would provide meat in the days ahead. The seal was somewhat of a disappointment. We boiled it but only got two gallons of oil. Not having salt, I preserved the skin with lime.

At seven o'clock on the morning of July 17, Max, Eric and Harold Brandt returned from a trek around the island to discover the *Helene* had broken her mooring. She was about three miles out to sea and moving away fast. Max and Eric jumped in their skiff and rowed over a wild sea for three hours before managing to board her. Max thought she had dragged her anchor, but when he tried to pull it in they discovered the anchor was gone. They were forced to hoist sail and battle the wind until they were close enough to shore to secure her lines. By this time it was six thirty in the evening. They bedded down for the night completely exhausted.

Following this incident, the *Helene* was secured by chains and anchor at both bow and stern. The Schlemmer party was then able to move about with some certainty that the fickle little craft would not desert them again. Their days were now devoted to making things more livable on the island; cleaning up waste and debris, burning rubbish and dead birds. There was only one chair on the island so Max found some scrap lumber and made two more chairs.

The Yacht Sloop *Helene*. Shown here in her glory days racing at Pearl Harbor

They also spent time killing rabbits, but that was not an easy task. When ammunition ran out, they resorted to catching them, then killing them with clubs or bare hands. Completely exterminating the rabbits proved to be an impossible task.

In late July, they were running out of water. A priority now was to dig a well. They started a well on August third; three days later they struck water. They now had a plentiful supply of water to meet their needs and this made life on the island easier.

One day in early August, they were overjoyed when they sighted 18 Laysan Teal racing about chasing flies. Birds of several different varieties were beginning to be seen on the island. At the same time, they watched the vicious attacks of the Frigate birds, the "pirates of the air" who were preying on the young terns, killing them by the hundreds. Not satisfied with destroying young terns on shore, these "pirates of the air" went after young fledglings in shoreline waters. In their frenzy, the Frigates would even attack sharks that were cruising for the same prey.

Female Frigate bird on nest. Laysan Island May 3, 1923.

Max could not stand by and watch the slaughter any longer. He told Eric and Harold to gather as many shotgun cartridges as they could. With shotguns loaded, Max and his posse crossed the island, shooting as they went. By sundown they had killed about 500 Frigate birds.

The party had now been ashore 58 days. Max's watch, the only timepiece on the island, had quit running. Time was now determined by the position of the sun. The weather had remained hot and sticky with the temperatures hovering between 90 and 100 degrees. The weather finally cooled down and they felt like working.

Max reports in his journal:

> Today we dug new holes and outhouses were set over them. We raised the lighthouse and stood it up in good position. There was a good rain yesterday. The wooden cistern that we sank into the ground just the other day, is half full of water. Eric went hunting this morning and brought home 14 plovers. We sorely needed a good meal.

The trio would take turns walking around the island several times a week. They kept a watchful eye on the shore for anything that might have washed up. They scanned the horizon constantly hoping to spot the *Thetis*, due at any time now by their reckoning. The ship would have much needed provisions for them, mail and perhaps, Max hoped, confirmation that he had been appointed to the position of Federal Warden for the Northwestern Bird Islands.

In the early evening of September 28th, a small boat appeared off the southwest point of the island. Max sent the boys off in a skiff to the harbor entrance to direct the craft through the reef safely.

Max raised the American flag atop the lighthouse and waited for a response from the crew. When there was none, Max got a gun and prepared to meet them fearing they might be poachers. Max wrote:

> I myself, took the shotgun and as the boat came very close and did not show any flag, I pointed my gun across the boat. I then noticed a man pulling an American flag out of a bag and holding it up in the air, at which I put down my gun and welcomed them. They landed on the beach where I found them to be a shipwrecked crew of the *O. M. Kellogg*, which got stranded on the night of the twenty fifth of September, at Maro Reef.

Aboard the boat were the Captain, his wife and the crew of the shipwrecked schooner. They had managed to bring aboard only a few provisions. The ship had left Apia, Samoa and was bound for San Francisco when it was stranded, three nights earlier on Maro Reef.

Besides Captain Charles A Lunn and his wife there were: First mate G.G. Treaner, Second Mate Antone Fretas, A.B. and donkeymen (Able bodied seamen and engine crew) John Bell, George Douglas, S. Silva and Harold Fatty. The cook was A. Tsukamoto, Cabin Boy Max Moss and Stewardess Julia Lynn.

Max was in a quandary as to what to do with the new island residents, eleven in all. He was short on provisions and had no way of knowing when the *Thetis* would arrive.

He decided the best course of action was to offer the *Helene* to Captain Lunn. The Captain and crew could make their way to Honolulu. Max would retrieve the *Helene* when he arrived there on the *Thetis*. Captain Lunn was also short on provisions and thought it best to wait a few days. Perhaps the *Thetis* would arrive in that time.

However, about a week later with no ship in sight, Captain Lunn and his First Mate, Treaner, decided to take the *Helene* to Midway, a shorter distance than Honolulu. Max raided his already short food supply and gave Captain Lunn all the bread, beans and corn beef he could spare. Max told them he would not charge for the use of the *Helene*, but, Max wrote that "I would hold him and the owners of the *O.M. Kellogg* responsible should there be any damage done to the boat-to pay for it. The Captain agreed to this effect and we signed the said agreement-me having the original he the duplicate."

On October 4th, at 10:55 A.M., the *Helene* with Captain Lunn, his wife and crew of the stranded *Kellogg* left her moorings at Laysan and set sail for Midway. A few days after the *Helene's* departure, Laysan was wracked by a powerful storm; lightening flashed and streaked along the limestone and sand and thunder crashed above. Max was sure the mighty force from the southwest would wash ashore some of the *Kellogg's* wreckage, especially food. It would arrive, but not for a while.

15

MAROONED, RESCUED, BETRAYED

When there was no word from Max since he sailed to Laysan on the *Helene* in June 1915, Therese wrote to Lt. Munter on the Coast Guard cutter *Thetis*. She asked him about the *Thetis's* planned trip to Laysan Island. Max had told her when he left Honolulu that the *Thetis* would be bringing them supplies and returning with news from them. (Her concern was justified as the *Thetis* never arrived at Laysan and Max was not safely home until December of that year.)

On October 16th, the weather cleared enough for Max and the boys to white-wash the buildings. But the project was soon abandoned as squalls continued to pass over the island. The three of them kept searching the shoreline for anything usable or eatable from the wreckage of the *Kellogg*.

Eric returned one day from fishing and proudly displayed a six-pound Moi. It was the first fish caught by hook and line. That same day the last tin of crackers was opened. On October 23rd, a pair of geese arrived at Laysan. This had never happened before. Unfortunately Max had to shoot them. He and the boys were desperate for food. He cut off their heads and feet so they could one day be identified.

In late October, Max began to worry about the Laysan Albatross. They should have arrived by now. So he was amazed one day when Eric announced the arrival of the first Gooneys. Throughout the years, the Albatross had arrived first, followed by the Gooneys. Max knew for sure then that the island bird cycle was out of whack. If the government would only listen to him, he lamented, he could straighten things out. The bird population was greatly depreciated. There were now 71 Gooneys and 10 Albatross ashore on the island. Since it was early November, there should have been two or three thousand of each species. There were just a few Laysan Terns; there should have been twenty or thirty thousand of them.

As the days wore on, the Gooney population increased to five hundred, the Albatross to three hundred. But it was a sad decrease from earlier years and a spectacle Max found hard to believe.

The days went slowly by, and still the *Thetis* did not arrive. The morale of Max's boys sunk very low. By the end of October, they had only flour, water and what little else they could scrounge. They were becoming weak and exhausted.

Then one day, Eric caught a large eel. It was five feet long and measured fifteen inches around. And as they expected, wreckage from the *Kellogg* began to wash ashore and the boys were overjoyed to find some tins of food amongst this wreckage. A few more turtles were captured and put in a dark room. On November 13th they found the first Gooney egg. Mixed with flour, it promptly became a meal of pancakes.

Three days later, the Stars and Stripes were raised to commemorate Therese Schlemmer's birthday. It became a real celebration when Eric and Harold came trudging up the beach with several tins of potatoes that had washed ashore. Bird eggs were plentiful now and they were boiled and pickled in brine.

Through November 17th and 18th, they were struck by a sandstorm that threatened to blow them away. When it finally passed, an eerie quiet fell on the island. Dead birds and rubbish had vanished and a new glaze of sand covered the island.

It was now late November. The sky was dark and overcast. The boys were terribly homesick. Max encouraged them to pray for God to send a ship. They were now into their last bag of flour. They strained their eyes out to sea, but no ship came into sight.

Max feared America might have become mixed up in the war, and if they were, he would gladly serve his new country no matter what.

It was now December 1915. The last three months had been hard on the boys. It was all Max could do to keep their courage up. Nothing could have prepared them for this. Day after day their eyes searched for the *Thetis*. But there was no *Thetis*, there never would be.

Early on the morning of December 2nd, while sifting worms out of the flour, Max saw the smoke from a steamer northwest from Laysan and heading in their direction. At once Eric and Harold began to literally jump for joy. Max had never seen a boy jump so high.

To be sure that the ship did not pass by the island, Max signaled the party's distress by hoisting the Stars and Stripes upside down. But there was no doubt of the ship's intention to dock. As it approached, the ship loomed up larger and larger and at last Max recognized it as the U.S.S. *Nereus*, a coal ship. Max watched in stark amazement as the monster of a ship entered Laysan harbor. It came in as near as any ship of smaller tonnage had ever come in before. As Max watch this spectacle, he muttered to the boys that this Captain knew his business. "A real number one!" he exclaimed.

Shortly before the appearance of the U.S.S. *Nereus* off the shore of Laysan Island, the ship was in port in Nagasaki, Japan, preparing to sail momentarily for Honolulu. The Commander of the U.S. Naval forces at Nagasaki received a cablegram from the Secretary of the Navy in Washington. The terse message read in part: "Proceed to Laysan Island and remove the inhabitants."

This order was then given to Captain Hutchinson, skipper of the *Nereus* who was told that there was a man, his son, and another man on Laysan Island and that they were trespassers. However, he didn't know that these trespassers were desperate to leave. Captain Hutchinson even feared that they might refuse to come with him so the Captain devised a plan. The ship was to drop anchor and go ashore with an invitation for the party to join them for lunch. If they refused to come to Honolulu, the ship would up anchor and get underway before they could get ashore.

As the *Nereus* got to the anchoring point, Max lowered the flag of distress and the ship dropped anchor. Max then hoisted the flag right side up. The shore party that arrived on the launch with Captain Hutchinson, included a young radio operator, named Harry Field. Harry was in the Naval Reserve and working his way though college to become an electrical engineer. (He was hired by Hawaiian Electric Company in 1926 and retired 32 years later as Commercial Vice President.) During these same years, Eric Schlemmer had become superintendent of the electrical contacting department of the Hawaiian Electric Company.

Harry remembered the encounter on Laysan Island in 1915 vividly and wrote about it in the July, 1967 issue of the *Hawaiian Electric Load Builder*.

> When Captain Hutchinson stepped ashore, Max Schlemmer shook the Captain's hand and fell to his knees, begging him to take Max and his men to Honolulu. I was amazed to see the courageous Captain Schlemmer on his knees.

Max told the captain that he was not expecting such a big ship, but that he was expecting either the schooner *Florence Ward* or the Coast Guard cutter *Thetis* and that he thought someone aboard would have orders for him. The Captain asked Max from whom he was expecting orders.

LAYSAN RESCUE

HARRY FIELD

Max explained that the Coast Guard ship *Thetis* was in Honolulu Harbor and was probably getting ready to head for Laysan right now. Max said the Executive

Officer of the *Thetis* probably had orders that told him he could exchange his men if they didn't want to stay any longer, but that Max should stay on to prevent bird pirating.

The Captain then told Max, rather pleasantly, that yes, he did have orders for him. The orders stated that Max was to go to Honolulu with the Captain. He said he had received orders from Commander of the U.S. Navy in Japan, who had received word from Washington, that Max, his son and the other man were trespassers on Laysan Island and that he was to bring them and all their belongings to Honolulu.

Max couldn't believe Washington wanted to take everybody away and turn the island over to bird pirates again. Max asked the Captain if perhaps there was a mistake in his message. He explained to the Captain that he thought he should probably remain, and send the other two back to Honolulu.

The Captain assured Max that his orders were to take everybody. Cold fury began to well up in Max. He had been set up. Someone wanted him out of the way and they got the U.S. Navy to do it for them. Max asked how much time there was for him and his men to get ready. The Skipper replied he would wait one day. Max told him they would be ready inside an hour.

Max wrote in his journal, "The Captain gave me his hand and said, 'Captain, you are a brick.'"

Max's anger had subsided somewhat. The thought occurred to him that he could possibly be going to Honolulu to sign some papers and be sworn in as Warden of the Bird Reservation.

Harry Field remembered the trip back to Honolulu and the fact that the boys just couldn't get enough to eat and that they consumed countless loaves of bread. With Captain Schlemmer and the boys aboard, the *Nereus* arrived at Honolulu Harbor on Sunday morning, December 5th, 1915.

Max was puzzled when a launch from the *Thetis* did not come out to meet their ship. He thought surely when he got ashore some of the officers would be on hand to greet him. But none were there.

Many Honolulu friends though, were there to greet him and the boys. No one had much to say. A customs officer asked Max if he had any freight on board. Captain Hutchinson quickly replied that "Yes, the man's freight is in the boat and everything is in order. I can vouch for that."

Max was next told that he and his men must remain aboard the *Nereus* until they were taken to see Mr. Sharp at the Customs house at 9 o'clock the next morning. However, Mr. Sharp later gave Max permission to go home and report back to him at 9 o'clock the next morning. Max sent the boys home but rather than go directly home himself, Max went aboard the *Thetis* and delivered his report. There was no order for him to sign papers; no mention about the position of Federal Warden of the Northwestern Bird Reservation.

It was an uncomfortable meeting. He was told there were some nasty rumors being circulated about him, but nobody believed them. They didn't tell Max what the rumors were about. When he got home, Therese told him that it was all over town that Max had a wireless radio on Laysan and was arrested as a German spy.

This is to certify that I Harold Brandt have this day Dec. 8, 1915 received from Max Schlemmer the sum of $187 one hundred eighty-seven dollars full amount of weighs due me from June 25, 1915. till Dec. 5, 1915 to and from Laysan Island

Harold Brandt

The next morning, Max, Eric and Harold Brandt reported to the U.S. Customs house where Max was interrogated. It was a galling experience for the King of Laysan. He had come to America forty-three years ago. There was no one more proud to be an American citizen than Max Schlemmer. Officers at U.S. Customs told Max they would write Washington and try to help him all they could. But they warned them that neither he nor the boys should attempt to leave Honolulu without first clearing it with them.

World War I was raging in Europe and anti-German feelings were running high. The fact that Max was born a citizen of Germany gave some validity to the spy rumor. Max called Harry Field to vouch for his loyalty, and put to rest the rumor of a wireless radio at Laysan; Harry went to Max's defense at once. Shortly thereafter word was received from Washington confirming that Max was not now, nor had he ever been, a German spy.

A disgruntled Max complained in his journal:

> As I went in good faith with the best of intentions to Laysan Island to help the government to do the right thing and preserve things, and worked very hard with my two men the whole time we were there. And I had to pay Harold Brandt, the sailor, $35.00 per month which was quite an expense for me and I had to buy provisions for my own boat which it was understood the government would later perhaps take over for themselves and pay me for it. Now as the said boat was wrecked at Midway Island, and I have not received any money yet from anywhere, I would kindly ask Congress and the American people at large whether this is any way to treat her citizens

Max was just now learning the fate of his sloop/yacht *Helene*.

He received the following letter from Lt. Munter, dated January 16, 1916:

My dear Mr. Schlemmer:

I have some bad news for you and I must say you have my sympathy. I only hope you may get something from the company that owns the *Kellogg* for the loss of your sloop yacht the *Helene*. The Captain has just received word from Mr. Morrison, superintendent of the cable station at Midway that they had a northwest storm, which caused the *Helene* to break adrift from her moorings and go aground, and swamp. He did not say whether she could be saved or not.

In regard to this matter, Captain Brown wishes me to extend his sympathy and assure you that if possible, all will be done by the *Thetis* to save your property when we go to Midway on the next cruise. As you know we are due to sail from the islands in the afternoon of the 18th of this month.

I advise you to get in touch with the owners of the *Kellogg* and find out what they want to do under the circumstances.

Believe me to be sincerely yours,

W. H. Munter

On January 25, 1916, a front page article in a Honolulu newspaper, titled "SLOOP HELENE LOST AT MIDWAY ISLAND, WIND IS HURRICANE" read as follows:

News of still another wreck was received in Honolulu yesterday. This time it is the Sloop *Helene*, owned by Max Schlemmer.

The captain received a cablegram from Midway Island yesterday that she went ashore Friday during a heavy westerly gale.

Breaking from her moorings, the *Helene* ran on the shoals, about one hundred yards from the cable pier and broke up Saturday afternoon. Some of the wreckage being washed up on the beach. The gale, then north northwest, continued Sunday, blowing at times with hurricane force, with occasional hail showers. This was the second time in thirteen years that hail has fallen in Midway, where the station of the Commercial Pacific Cable Company is located.

The Sloop and Max Schlemmer have had adventure a plenty since June when the Captain sailed for Laysan Island. The schooner *O.M. Kellog* was wrecked on Maro Reef in September and the crew made Laysan in the ship's boat. At Laysan, the men borrowed the Sloop from Schlemmer to go to Midway whence they were brought to the United States by the Navy tug *Iroquois* which made a special voyage for them. Schlemmer and his two companions were taken from Laysan by the United States Navy collier *Nereus* in November.

New mooring buoys were planted by the *Iroquois* when she was at Midway for mooring the *Helene*.

This report of bad weather at Midway proves that the Pacific is not all pacific these days. Gales near the coast, at the islands north of Fiji and at Midway show general bad weather.

Max was sure that both man and God were conspiring against him. The *Helene* was a total loss. And it would be difficult to prove that the loss of the *Helene* had been caused by negligence. Midway, which lies well out of the tropic zone, is subject to sudden and violent storms, especially during the winter.

Max was very distraught and had no idea what to do about the loss. He was advised to hire an attorney, which he did. His attorney in Honolulu contacted

Atkins, Kroll and Co. in San Francisco, who represented the owners of the *Kellogg*. On May 11, 1916 Max received a letter written aboard the S.S. *Matsonia* by attorney Kroll.

The letter explained that when the U.S.S. *Iroquois* arrived at Midway to take Captain Lunn and crew to Honolulu, the Captain of the U.S. Government tug told Captain Lunn he could do nothing about the *Helene* and that he approved of her mooring place as being the safest place for her to be. The letter further explained that when Captain Lunn arrived in Honolulu he could get no instructions from the people to whom he had been referred by you. He had no alternative in the matter except to explain the situation to the government officials. This he did.

Since Max's instructions were complied with and every precaution had been taken for the safety of the *Helene* at Midway, the owners refused to assume any responsibility for her loss. However, in view of the services rendered to the Captain and crew, the owners of the *O.M. Kellogg* offered Max the sum of $500.00. Max had no choice other than to accept it. If he refused, attorney's fees would be astronomical. He would have to sue each individual shareholder for their portion of the claim, and there were a lot of them living in different parts of the country.

16

THE TWILIGHT YEARS

The once proud Captain Schlemmer, King of Laysan Island, had to face reality. He was broke. He was now sixty years old. By this time, he and Therese had nine children; Pinkham Laysan was born January 2, 1914 in Honolulu and Helene Wilhelmina's birth followed on January 9, 1916, also in Honolulu. The three children from his first wife remained on Kauai with their grandparents.

The sole means of their support, the yacht *Helene*, now a pile of wreckage, lay deep in the Pacific Ocean at Midway. Max was in desperate need of help. The help arrived from James D. Levenson, an acquaintance who admired Max Schlemmer and had followed his adventuresome career through all its high points and low points. Levenson wrote a letter to the community at large and to some of the organizations with whom Max had been affiliated such as the Odd Fellows and the Masons.

Levenson wrote the following letter, dated February 7, 1916:

Gentlemen:

As you are aware, our fellow townsman, Mr. Max Schlemmer, has recently been returned from Laysan Island, which is one of the group of small islands forming the Hawaiian Island Bird Reservation and therefore under the jurisdiction of the U. S. Biological Survey. Owing to the timely and generous assistance rendered by Mr. Schlemmer to the ten members of the shipwrecked crew of the *O. M. Kellogg* last September and the use of his vessel by them which was left by these unfortunate people at Midway, he is back in Honolulu without his vessel and without employment.

There should be a warden stationed on Laysan to guard at all seasons the wonderful bird colonies there from further depredations and to assist shipwrecked and distressed vessels in the windward chain of islands. There is reason to hope that the Biological Survey will soon supplement the work of the *Thetis* and appoint a regular resident warden for this great bird reservation. It is to be

89

hoped that Mr. Schlemmer will receive this position since it is one he is well fitted to fill. But in the meantime, Mr. Schlemmer and his family are in need of
temporary help. I therefore bring this matter to your attention, trusting that you
will respond and assist this man who has lived long in these islands and in this
instance, as well as in others that need not be mentioned, has rendered assistance of such a nature that the community should not be willing to see him suffer as a result of his humane acts on Laysan.

Please make your check payable to Max Schlemmer, and mail same in the
enclosed envelope. Mr. Schlemmer will send acknowledgments personally.

Very truly yours

James D. Levensaon
Honolulu

P.S. Above all Mr. Schlemmer wants employment and will be obliged if you can
furnish him work or tell him where he can find a temporary or permanent job

In spite of the fact that war was raging in Europe and sentiment was on the
rise against Germans in Hawaii and America, substantial funds began arriving for
the Schlemmers.

Along with these charitable acts, the well-known German company H. Hackfeld, hired Max to be the superintendent of their offices in downtown Honolulu
at the H. Hackfeld building. Max Schlemmer was a prominent name in the
annals of H. Hackfeld and Company. At long last it appeared as though Max had
escaped the ravages of fate. He was gainfully employed. Therese saw that their
funds were wisely invested in real estate. A few of the older children were now
able to contribute to the family's support. Surely peace, and tranquility had
found its way to their Kalihi home.

Germany's unrestricted submarine warfare brought America into the war
against Germany on April 6, 1917. Although the Schlemmers were not enemy
aliens, they were Germans nevertheless and were restricted to Oahu.

The Schlemmer children endured taunts from other children who often threw
stones at them on their way to school. The Schlemmers found one sympathetic
family in their Kalihi neighborhood; the Fongs, a poor Chinese family, became
their good friends. Hiram Fong and my Mother, Ottilie remained lifelong
friends. (Hiram in later years built a financial empire on Oahu and became the
first person of Asian decent to be elected to the United States Congress.)

The Schlemmer family, 1916. Front row: Adele, Eric, Max holding Pinkham, Grandma Therese holding Helene, Eva, Otto, Regina. Back row: Therese, Ottilie, Ida.

There were no such friends for German businesses or cultural organizations. They were seized by Richard H. Trent on behalf of the U.S. Alien Property Custodian. After a pittance was paid, H. Hackfeld and Co. and its subsidiary, B.F. Ehlers, became the properties of the American and British stockholders. H. Hackfeld Co. was renamed American Factors (AMFAC), B.F. Ehlers became Liberty House. The German school at Lihue was closed and never reopened.

By 1922, the Schlemmer family in Honolulu had increased by three; Edward Henry, born January 23, 1918, Norman David, born February 6, 1920 and my aunt Lorraine Estelle, born September 14, 1922. She is nine months older than I am.

Max was satisfied with his job at the AMFAC building, now under American and British ownership. Several years later, however, Max fell though an open elevator shaft and was seriously injured. After several month's recuperation, Max was able to return to work. As the years went on, his health began failing, perhaps as a result of this accident. The King of Laysan was retired in 1927. His pension was $100.00 a month.

Max, the old sea Captain, remained in Honolulu moored to the front porch of his home at Wilder Avenue. It seems a bit of irony that this street, Wilder Avenue, bears the name of Samuel Gardner Wilder, shipping magnate and former Minister of the Interior, whose son Garrit P. Wilder was now the Federal Warden of the Hawaiian Islands Bird Reservation, the position Max had coveted most of his life.

In later years, Therese managed the household and family matters. I vividly recall my grandmother driving a big Studebaker around town on her errands and shopping. Therese died two years after Max, on January 11, 1937. She was 58 years old.

During their 45 year marriage, Therese, even at a young age, was always solicitous for Max's well being. She worried when he was at sea because he couldn't swim. In her quiet way, Therese coped with all family matters and problems. Max was shielded from any controversy and the last years of his life were serene. He spent the days "talking story" and reminiscing. It was here at Wilder Avenue that my grandfather died in 1935 at the age of seventy-nine.

17

THE TANAGER EXPEDITION

The story of Max Schlemmer would not be complete without mention of the Tanager Expedition of 1923. The introduction of rabbits onto the minuscule Hawaiian Island of Laysan in 1902 by my grandfather Max, led to the devastation and almost total ruin, of the island's flora and fauna. But twenty-one years elapsed, before officials in Washington D.C. took any action in this regard.

In 1909, President Theodore Roosevelt had placed the far-flung group of Hawaiian Islands, including Laysan, under federal protection. These islands were henceforth known as the Hawaiian Islands Bird Reservation and were to be administered by the U.S. Biological Survey, Washington D.C.

Another fourteen years went by and still the federal government had done little if anything to protect or care for the islands. Rabbits continued to multiply and munch to the devastation of the islands' ecosystems. The Japanese continued to violate U.S. Territorial rights in this area and to slaughter birds for their valuable plumage.

Early in 1923, Dr. Herbert E. Gregory, director of the Bishop Museum in Honolulu realized that something must be done to put an end to this wanton destruction taking place within the U.S. Territory of Hawaii. He contacted E.W. Nelson, Chief of the U.S. Biological Survey in Washington and strongly advised him that immediate steps must be taken to protect these islands. Nelson immediately went to his superior, Henry Wallace, Secretary of Agriculture, briefed him on the situation and suggested that he, Nelson, be allowed to formulate a plan to protect this Hawaiian Bird Reservation and to put the plan into action. Nelson suggested that an expedition be undertaken as a fact-finding mission relative to the Bureau of Biological Survey's caretaker role as guardian of the Bird Reservation.

Nelson was also aware that rabbits introduced onto Laysan Island, had caused serious ecological damage and so the elimination of the rabbits became an important stated goal. Secretary Wallace concurred with Nelson's plan and authorized him to proceed.

In the meantime, Henry Wallace was able to enlist the Navy's assistance to furnish transportation and other support at their disposal, for the expedition. The value of such a mission was recognized by the Acting Chief of Naval Operations and he added the islands of Johnson and Wake to the itinerary. In Hawaii, the Navy assigned the *Tanager*, a World War minesweeper, the task of providing transportation for the expedition. Thus the expedition got its name Tanager.

Atoll Research Bulletin Nos. 432/434 states, "The primary objective of both the Biological Survey and the Bishop Museum, however, was a thorough biological reconnaissance of the islands, including documentation by adequate series of specimens of terrestrial and marine organisms. The expedition was not without benefit to the Navy as well, through gathering navigational and other data of military use."

And so the mission of the Tanager Expedition had been expanded from a rabbit hunt to include collecting as many species of birds, mammals and fish as time allowed. All species were to be preserved, packed and sent to the Bureau in Washington with a few species being sent to Bishop Museum in Honolulu. All islands, islets, reefs etc. were to be given a name.

With much fanfare, the Tanager Expedition left Honolulu aboard the *Tanager*, April 4. 1923. The *Tanager* was under the command of Captain Stephen Ingham. They arrived at Laysan Island three days later.

The *Tanager* was to make three round trips between these islands in the Hawaiian Bird Reservation and Honolulu. The Commandant of the 14th Naval District, Admiral Simpson named Commander Samuel W. King special representative for the Navy and to act as a liaison in seeing that the expedition was given every consideration within the Navy's power to do so. Sam King, a native Hawaiian and an Annapolis graduate, was appointed Governor of the Territory of Hawaii thirty years later, governing from 1953 to 1957.

Nelson himself, a renowned mammalogist and ornithologist, appointed Alexander Wetmore to lead the expedition. Wetmore was recognized by the Smithsonian Institution as one of the leading ornithologists of the 20th century. Charles E. Reno, a Biological Assistant of the Survey in Phoenix, Arizona, joined the expedition as a pest control expert to oversee the rabbit extermination program. In a letter to Reno in February 1923, Nelson emphasized that the destruction of the rabbit population on all the islands of the Bird Reservation, was an important matter. He wrote:

I hope you will be able to actually exterminate the last rabbit on the island during the month which can be devoted to that purpose. Failure to do so will be a great disappointment to me and would necessitate another effort at considerable expense. We have arranged to have 75 ounces of strychnine sent to you directly at Phoenix for use on this trip.

You will find it necessary to arrange in San Francisco for the purchase and transportation of from one to two tons of best grade bailed alfalfa for use in poison operations. In addition you will need to purchase at least two single shot 22 rifles and perhaps twelve thousand or fifteen thousand rounds of 22-caliber ammunition for use in killing rabbits. Other measures for the extermination of these animals will probably suggest themselves to you and can be arranged for.

Tanager Expedition Members, left to right: Sam King, A.J. Ker, G. Grant, A. Wetmore, D.R. Dickey, D. Fullaway, S.C. Ball, E.L. Caum, D. Thaanum, C.E. Reno, E.Schlemmer, Lt. L Cdr. T. Wilson, J.W. Thompson. A.J Ker, pictured above was not a member of the expedition. He was an employee of the cable company returning to Midway after sick leave on Oahu.

Dr. Wetmore recruited a number of scientists, and other experts in their field, including my uncle, twenty-year-old Eric Schlemmer, an expert on Laysan Island. Eric was Max's son, born on the island and had been there often as a young teenager. He knew the habits of the wild life; the nesting areas and flight patterns of the birds. He was also the expedition's "reef pilot."

Eric was hired to accompany the expedition party on all three trips of the Tanager Expedition. Donald R. Dickey, the official photographer wrote in his journal a bit about each member of the first party.

About Eric, he wrote: "We also have Eric Schlemmer, a son of the Max Schlemmer, whose name is indelibly associated with the island of Laysan, as guano manager, rabbit importer, etc.! The boy goes as my camera assistant."

Eric Laysan Schlemmer, known in his early years as the "Prince of Laysan."

As Eric and Dickey walked around the island one day, they came upon a group of five big Green Turtles. Dickey took motion pictures of Eric "rollin them over." Eric had been given the nickname "roll 'em over, Eric." Dickey wrote,

"They are helpless on their backs, but the big ones are fiends to turn. Brought in a small one of perhaps 50 lbs. to eat."

Besides being camera assistant to Dickey during the first stop at Laysan, Eric helped Reno with the rabbit extermination mission. They filled rabbit burrows with poisoned alfalfa and sometimes poisoned sweet potatoes. Together, they roamed the island with loaded shotguns and on good days, could kill as many as 50 rabbits in a few hours.

On the second trip, Dr. Wetmore announced that "Eric Schlemmer will be my assistant from now on." Eric helped to prepare the bird skins and pack the specimens for shipment to Washington. Wetmore also spent some time teaching Eric the art of skinning the birds.

Eric could always be counted on to provide food from the sea. Dickey wrote in his journal: "Schlemmer and the Filipino boy have just come in with 30 crawfish and an eel to show for two hours of 'jacking' and 'spearing' on the reef."

Besides hunting and killing rabbits, the party collected and preserved a sizable amount of wild life specimen. Eight boxes containing seal skulls and skeletons, sealskins, bird skeletons and eggs, small bird and mammal skins as well as salted bird skins, were loaded aboard the ship. From Honolulu they were sent to Washington D.C.

The expedition completed its first round trip early in May. When the *Tanager* left on its second trip, a number of so-called volunteers were aboard, led by Gerrit P. Wilder, the Federal Warden for the Hawaiian Bird Reservation. Joining the party among others was Lorrin A. Thurston, owner of the *Honolulu Advertiser*, Theodore Dranga, shell collector, John Baker, a Hawaiian fish collector and Austin Jones, along for the fishing trip.

On June 9, 1923, the *Tanager* left Honolulu on the last leg of its mission for the Bureau of the Biological Survey. Dr. Wetmore, Uncle Eric and three others were all that remained of the original Tanager party. A new group of volunteers joined the party, led by C.S. Judd, Executive Officer of the Hawaii Board of Agriculture, and including Bruce Cartwright of the Hawaii Historical Society, Dr. C. Montague Cooke, a conchologist, interested in land shells, Edwin H. Bryan, entomologist from the Bishop Museum, ALC Atkinson, interested in Heiaus on Necker, and W. G. Anderson, sailor and fisherman.

By the completion of the Tanager Expedition, one of its most important missions had been accomplished: the rabbits on Laysan Island had been exterminated. The expedition ended on July 1, 1923, as the *Tanager* returned to Honolulu after its third trip to the Hawaiian Bird Reservation.

Uncle Eric steadfastly maintained till the day he died that "if the Navy had not kicked us off the island, my Dad and I could have gotten rid of the rabbits on Laysan Island." By allowing fourteen years to pass before taking action, the U.S. Government must shoulder some blame for the depredation of what was once the "greatest bird island in the world."

J. B. Mann plotting soundings with Commander Sam King.

EPILOGUE

So far as it is known, Captain Max Schlemmer was, until his death, the oldest man still living in Hawaii who had been an active whaler in the Pacific and Arctic waters. Max, the old sea captain, remained in Honolulu until his death.

There were those who determined to see that evil would not live after him nor the good be buried with his bones. In far off Seattle, Washington, August Toeller, now a judge, had been with Max and Therese on Laysan during some of their darkest days, after the death, at birth, of their firstborn child, Adam. Toeller wrote an article in the Duwamish Valley Newspaper in praise of the life of Max Schlemmer. The final paragraph read:

> In the death of Captain Schlemmer there went out from this life, one of the kindliest gentlemen it was my pleasure ever to have known. He was tolerant to the fault, charitable, to the weaker of both sexes, a stern Captain when in charge of men on the island or at sea, a loveable husband, a wonderful father, a friend loyal and true, a servant faithful and obedient, a citizen who loved the flag, a neighbor who plugged for his community and a believer in truth and righteousness that made him outstanding among men.

Max fathered seventeen children, of whom fifteen lived to adulthood. His first wife, Auguste had three children and Therese had fourteen.

Max's daughter Therese Bredehoft wrote the following eulogy to her father, with perhaps a nod to Walt Whitman:

OUR CAPTAIN

Oh Captain! Our Captain
What strange wind blows thy sail,
It seems, oh beloved skipper
To carry you out beyond the pale.
In vain we try to reach you once more
For one last caress before you leave our shore
But our feeble craft must continue to be

Off here to traverse this life's great sea.
The least we can do is our best—to make
The Great Master proud for your dear sake
And we'll sail with stout hearts and love
The mate of your good ship, our Mother.
While an angel's choir takes up our refrain
Oh God be with you till we meet again.

Honolulu's newspapers had always considered Max "good copy," and they were not about to desert him now. The headline in the *Hawaiian Star* was: CAPTAIN MAX SCHLEMMER, LINK WITH WHALING DAYS, SAILS ON." The article read:

Eighty years of a sturdy sailor's life—63 of it at sea—ended early this morning when Maximillian Schlemmer sailed into the unknown port from the family home at 1817 Wilder Ave. For three score years and ten he had followed the sea. He started as a youngster raw from Germany, lonely, determined to be a master mariner. He ended his seafaring days as a captain of trading schooners in Hawaiian waters and devoted guardian of island properties in the great chain that stretches northwest from Oahu and Kauai. In the heyday of his busy life they called him the "King of Laysan." Hardships at sea, including the loss of a vessel on the grinding coral reef of Laysan Island took their toll on the sturdy sailor's physique. For some years prior to his death, he had broken down in his nerves. He had returned from the sea, but the sea was always in his blood. In his last months his talk and thoughts were often far away, out where the Pacific bellows, where the trade winds and sea birds have long been his companions.

APPENDIX

Max's Police Constable's commission from Kingdom of Hawaii

Bernice Pauahi Bishop Museum
of
Polynesian Ethnology and Natural History.

Mr May Schlemmer   Honolulu, H.I.

Dear Sir,

        I am directed by a note of the Trustees of
the Bernice Pauahi Bishop Museum to acknowledge
the receipt of your Gift to the Museum, and to
return to you their thanks for the same.

                                        I have the honor to be
                                        With great respect,
                                        Very truly yours,

                                        Wm J. Brigham

A fine collection of
Nests and Eggs
from Laysan Id.

A letter thanking Max for some birds and eggs that were sent to Bishop Museum

U.S.S. Albatross,
Laysan, May 17th 1902.

Dear Sir:-

Professor Nutting tells me of your patriotic feelings regarding the flag and I assure you they are highly appreciated. In our service we hoist our colors in port at 8 o'clock in the morning. The Army hoists theirs at sunrise.

Page 1 of a letter from Cmdr. Chauncey Thomas, skipper of the *Albatross* after Max had asked some questions about the flag ceremony

Page 2 and 3 of letter from Cmdr. Thomas

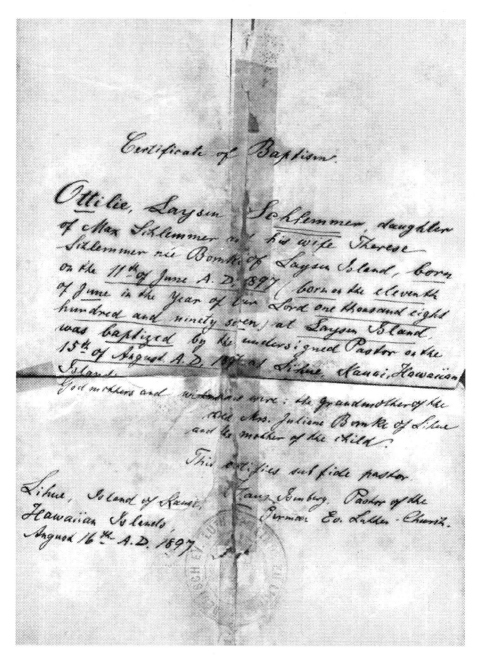

My mother Ottilie's Certificate of baptism

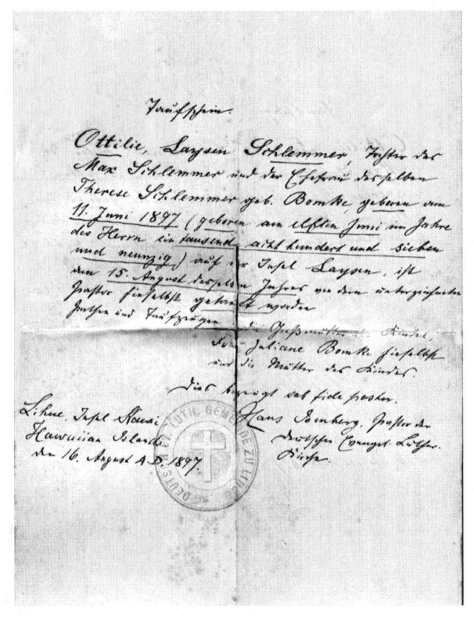

Back of Ottilie's Certificate of baptism

Page 1 of a 3 page letter to Max's wife Therese from Adele, Dr Hugo H.
Schauinsland's wife.

you & your husband have so
well provided for us during our
staying there, we will never forget it. As soon we will have picture
of us, we will send you some. The
present ones are not well made.
Perhaps you also would favor
us with your pictures.

That you kept Minna on the
Island was very usfull for you.
At present Minna will probably
be at home or in Honolulu.

Our voyage was beautifull
& smoothly, but at times
very sauer. My husband had to
overcome some hardship, & me
with him. The end good, all good,
so we reached our Germany again
after 1¼ years & specially our two
children, who came to fuck us
at the Station of Görlitz, grown up
quit a bit. Never will I forget
the moment, when we opened the
car door, rushing out & were
standing in front of our children
Martha, the older will be 9 years

Page 2 of the letter

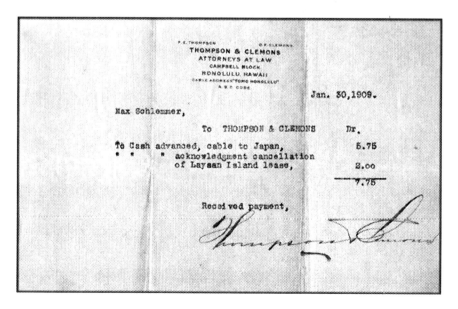

Last page of the letter. It was written on the back of a chart from
Hawaii's Mission Acadamy poultry breeding farm that you can see
bleeding through the letter

Receipt for cable to Japan about loss of lease for Laysan 1909

HONOLULU, MAY 14th, 1904.

E. R. STACKABLE ESQUIRE,

Collector of Customs, Honolulu,

Dear Sir:-

I beg to call your attention to the fact th
certain Japanese are at present encamped without authority on th
Island of Lysianski, belonging to the United States Government.
These men are destroying the birds upon said island and otherwis
committing havoc there and have been repeatedly warned to leave
the island. Said Island is leased by the Pacific Guano and Ferti
lizer Company, and I as Agent of said Company protest against sai
Japanese remaining on the Island of Lysianski in contravention o
the rights of said Company and I ask that you use all your endea
to have said Japanese removed from the island. I have spoken up
this matter to Captain Niblack, U. S. N. who referred me to you
the proper person in the premises.

Yours truly,

(Signed) Max Schlemmer

Copy of letter sent to E R Stackable
my 14th 1904

Letter warning about bird poaching in 1904
Note the watermark at top of letter.

THE UNITED STATES OF AMERICA.

Sections 4170, 4171, 4192, 4195, 4194, 4196, and 4197, Revised Statutes.

Cat. No. 518.

BILL OF SALE OF ENROLLED VESSEL.

To all to whom these Presents shall come, Greeting:

know ye, That A L L E N & R O B I N S O N , L I M I T E D ,
a Corporation duly organized under the laws of the Territory of Hawaii,
with principal place of business at Honolulu, said territory,

owners
of the _____ **Schooner** _____ or vessel, called the _____ **"Luka"**

of the burden of _____ **Seventy** _____ tons or thereabout,
for and in consideration of the sum of _____ **Ten (10-)** _____
_____ dollars,
lawful money of the United States of America, to ____ **it** ____ in hand paid, before the sealing and delivery
of these presents, by: _____ **Theresa Schlemmer, wife of Max Schlemmer, of** _____
Honolulu, Territory of Hawaii, _____

the receipt whereof ____ **it** ____ does hereby acknowledge and ____ **is** ____ therewith fully satisfied, contented, and
paid, have bargained and sold, and by these presents do bargain and sell, unto the said : **Theresa** _____
Schlemmer, her _____

executors, administrators, and assigns, ____ **the whole** _____
of the said _____ **Schooner** _____ or vessel, together with the ____ **all of**

Front of the Bill of Sale for the *Luka*

Enrollment No. 62.

OFFICIAL NUMBER.
VESSELS	LETTER.
141,652

ENROLLMENT.

In conformity to Title L, "Regulation of Vessels in Domestic Commerce," of the Revised Statutes of the United States, **S. W. Spencer of Honolulu, Secretary** having taken and subscribed the **oath** required by law, and having **sworn** that **Allen & Robinson Ltd., a corporation organized and existing under the laws of the Territory of Hawaii, is**

citizen of the United States, and the sole owner of the vessel called the **" L U K A "** of **Honolulu**, whereof **Kalua**, a citizen of the United States, is master, and that the said vessel was built in the year **1878**, at **Port Ludlow, Washington** as appears by **P. E. #14 issued at Honolulu, Aug. 9, 1900, now surrendered. Owners changed.**

and **said enrollment** having certified that the said vessel is a **schooner** built of **wood**, that she has **one** deck **two** masts, head, stern; that her length is **77.** feet, her breadth **23.** feet, her depth **8.** feet, her height feet; that she measures as follows:

	TONS.	100THS.
Capacity under tonnage deck	122	35
Capacity between decks above tonnage deck		
Capacity of inclosures on the upper deck, viz:		
GROSS TONNAGE	122	35
Deductions under Section 4153, Revised Statutes, as amended by Act of March 2, 1895:		
Crew space, ; Master's cabin, ;		
Steering gear, ; Anchor gear, ;		
Boatswain's stores, ; Chart house, ; Storage of sails, ;		
Donkey engine and boiler, ; Propelling power, ;		
TOTAL DEDUCTIONS		
NET TONNAGE	70	

That the following-described spaces, and no others, have been omitted, viz:

and said vessel has been duly enrolled at the Port of

Given under my hand and seal at the Port of **Honolulu** in

Back of the Bill of Sale for the *Luka*

U. S. S. IROQUOIS,

Honolulu, T. H.,

April 18, 1905.

S I R :-

1. Referring to our conversation of the other day, I understand that the Cable Company has 70 tons of stores to go to Midway, and I will have about 25 tons for the IROQUOIS to take. I wish to take a lot of soil for gardening purposes, and I would like to negotiate with the schooner LEVI WOODBURY to take such part of my cargo as I may designate, for the consideration that I will tow the schooner to Midway Island, and subsequently to Laysan, leaving her at the latter island, the schooner to take all risks. Please call and see me at your earliest convenience.

Very respectfully,

A.P.Niblack

Lieut.Commander, U.S.N.,

Commanding IROQUOIS & Station.

Captain Max Schlemmer,

Honolulu, T. H.

Letter from the Skipper of the *Iroquois* to Max about towing the *Levi Woodbury* to Laysan Island 1905

EXECUTIVE BUILDING
SECRETARY OF HAWAII

HONOLULU, T. H., August 10/07.

My dear Captain:-

As Arthur Brown is up on Molokai and the "Iroquois"
is leaving today, and will call at your Island, I
take this opportunity in writing you.

The "Luka" left here on June 30th, and has not
yet arrived.   I am a little bit worried about it.

I am sending by the "Iroquois" some apples, pine-
apples, oranges and other fruit for yourself and
family.   I hope that you will enjoy some fresh
fruit.

Captain Carter of the "Iroquois" is going to visit
all the Islands in search of shipwreck crews.   I am
also sending you a file of papers.

I hope that you are in the best of health and
that everything is all right with the "Luka".

Your friend,

P. S.   Brown has just arrived from Molokai on
the "Kinau" but will not have time to write.   He
told me to give you his regards.

Letter expressing concern for the whereabouts of the *Luka*.

HONOLULU,   HAWAII   December7th 1908

Messrs. Thompson & Clemons,
        Honolulu, Hawaii.

Gentlemen:-

In the matter of the lease of Laysan and Lesiansky Islands in the Pacific Ocean, as I am not likely to be in the Territory of Hawaii at the time when the said lease will be put up at auction, by the Government, I hereby authorize your firm, or Mr. F.E.Thompson or Mr. Charles F.Clemons to bid at said auction in my name and behalf as follows: An offer of $25.oo per annum rental over and above the Royalty of fifty cents (50¢) per long ton of guano shipped from said islands and an agreement to plant or set out five hundred (500) cocoanut trees per annum.

In case other bidders should offer more than $25.oo per annum rental I hereby authorize you or either of you to bid in my name and behalf as high as $100.oo per annum, but not in excess thereof. But in case I should instruct you by cable or otherwise before said auction sale to bid any other sum or in excess of said $100.oo you are to bid in my name and behalf as so directed.

Max Schlemmer

Witness:

Thos L Seybolt

Letter from Max to his agent giving authorization to bid for the lease of Laysan and Lisiansky Islands

EXECUTIVE ORDER.

It is hereby ordered that the following islets and reefs, name-
ly: Cure Island, Pearl and Hermes Reef, Lysianski or Pell Island,
Mary Reef, Laysan Island, Dowsetts Reef, Gardiner Island, Two Brothers Reef, French Frigate Shoal, Necker Island, Frost Shoal and Bird
Island, situated in the Pacific Ocean at and near the extreme western
extension of the Hawaiian Archipelago between latitudes twenty-three
degrees and twenty-nine degrees north, and longitudes one hundred
and sixty degrees and one hundred and eighty degrees west from Green-
wich, and located within the area segregated by the broken lines
shown upon the diagram hereto attached and made a part of this order,
are hereby reserved and set apart, subject to valid existing rights,
for the use of the Department of Agriculture as a preserve and breeding ground for native birds. It is unlawful for any person to hunt,
trap, capture, wilfully disturb, or kill any bird of any kind whatever, or take the eggs of such birds within the limits of this reservation, except under such rules and regulations as may be pre-
scribed from time to time by the Secretary of Agriculture. Warning
is expressly given to all persons not to commit any of the acts herein enumerated and which are prohibited by law.
    This reservation to be known as the Hawaiian Islands Reservation.

                                    THEODORE ROOSEVELT.

THE WHITE HOUSE,
    February 3, 1909.

                    -(No. 1019.)-

                U.S. NAVAL STATION,
                    HONOLULU, T.H.
                    June 7, 1909.

            GENERAL ORDER.

    The Commandant of the Naval Station, Hawaii, has been authoriz-
ed by the Secretary of the Navy, to carry the above Executive Order
into effect, and the Naval forces at his command or within his requisition will be used, if necessary, for the maintenance of the law
governing the preservation of birds and the immunity of their breeding ground in the Hawaiian Islands Reservation.

                            Captain, U.S.Navy,
                                Commandant.

The Executive order that stopped Max's lease

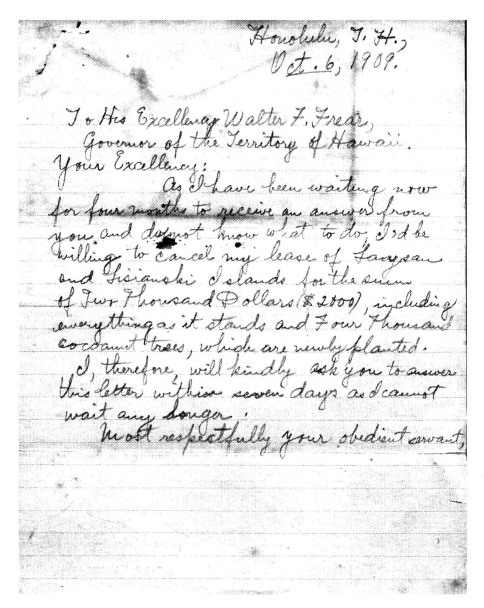

Honolulu, T. H.,
Oct. 6, 1909.

To His Excellency Walter F. Frear,
Governor of the Territory of Hawaii.
Your Excellency:
            As I have been waiting now
for four months to receive an answer from
you and do not know what to do, I'd be
willing to cancel my lease of Laysan
and Lisianski Islands for the sum
of Two Thousand Dollars ($2000), including
everything as it stands and Four Thousand
coconut trees, which are newly planted.
    I, therefore, will kindly ask you to answer
this letter within seven days as I cannot
wait any longer.
        Most respectfully, your obedient servant,

An offer from Max to Governor Frear to cancel his lease

October 7, 1909.

Mr. Max Schlemmer,

    Honolulu, T. H.

Dear Sir:

    Replying to your letter of the 6th instant, in which you state that you would be willing to cancel your lease of Laysan and Lisianski islands for $2,000, the Territory of course cannot pay you for a cancellation of the lease; indeed, it is immaterial to the Territory whether the lease is cancelled or not. What view the authorities in Washington take as to the validity of the lease they have not yet indicated.

    Respectfully yours,

        Governor.

Governor's reply to Max's letter on previous page

Executive Chamber.
Honolulu, Hawaii

November 30, 1909.

Mr. Max Schlemmer,

Honolulu, T. H.

Dear Sir:

I have to inform you that we have received advices from the Secretary of Interior that the Commissioner of Public Lands of the Territory was on February 8, 1909, without jurisdiction or authority to execute the lease of that deed to you of the islands of Laysan and Lysianski, an executive order having been made by the President of the United States on February 3, 1909, which appropriated these islands to the use and purposes of the federal government. It has been held by the Secretary of Interior that such appropriation terminated territorial control; at least, to the extent that the Territory was without authority to execute said lease to you.

You are therefore requested to return your copy of the lease, in order that cancellation thereof may be duly entered upon our records.

Very respectfully,

E. A. Mott Smith.

Acting Governor.

Official termination of lease letter

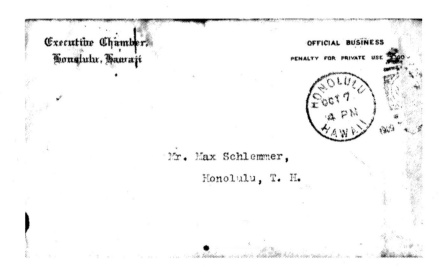

Envelope letter came in. Note that the envelope marked OFFICIAL
BUSINESS much the same as we have today

Receipt for a small boat before last trip to Laysan Island

Bill of Sale.

TO ALL TO WHOM THESE PRESENTS SHALL COME, greeting.

KNOW ye, that I, GEORGE TAIT, of Honolulu, Territory of Hawaii, sole owner of the ~~sloop Yacht "HELENE"; of the burden of _____tons or thereabout, lying at Pearl Harbor, Hawaiian Islands, for and in consideration of the sum of FOUR HUNDRED ($400.~) DOLLARS, lawful money of the United States of America, to me in hand paid by MAX JOSEPH AUGUST SCHLEMMER, of Bieber, Lassen County, State of California, receipt whereof is hereby acknowledged, and the further consideration of the assumption, by the said MAX JOSEPH AUGUST SCHLEMMER, of debts against the said Sloop Yacht "HELENE" amounting to but not to exceed TWO HUNDRED and SEVENTY-FIVE ($275.00) DOLLARS, as per list of creditors bills filed and agreed to between the parties hereto, have bargained and sold, and by these presents do bargain and sell, unto the said MAX JOSEPH AUGUST SCHLEMMER, his executors, administrators, and assigns, a l l of the said Sloop Yacht "HELENE" now lying in Pearl Harbor, together with all the masts, bowsprit, sails, boats, anchors, cables, tackle, furniture, Nautical Instruments, tools, stores and all other necessaries thereto appertaining and belonging, excepting, only, the clothing of the men and crew.

TO HAVE AND TO HOLD the said Sloop Yacht "HELENE" and appurtenances thereunto belonging unto him the said MAX JOSEPH AUGUST SCHLEMMER, his executors, administrators, and assigns, forever; and I, the said GEORGE TAIT, have, and by these presents do promise, covenant, and agree, for myself, my heirs, executors, administrators, and assigns, to WARRANT and DEFEND the said Sloop Yacht "HELENE" and all the other before mentioned appurtenances against a l l and every person and persons whomsoever.

Bill of Sale for the *Helene*

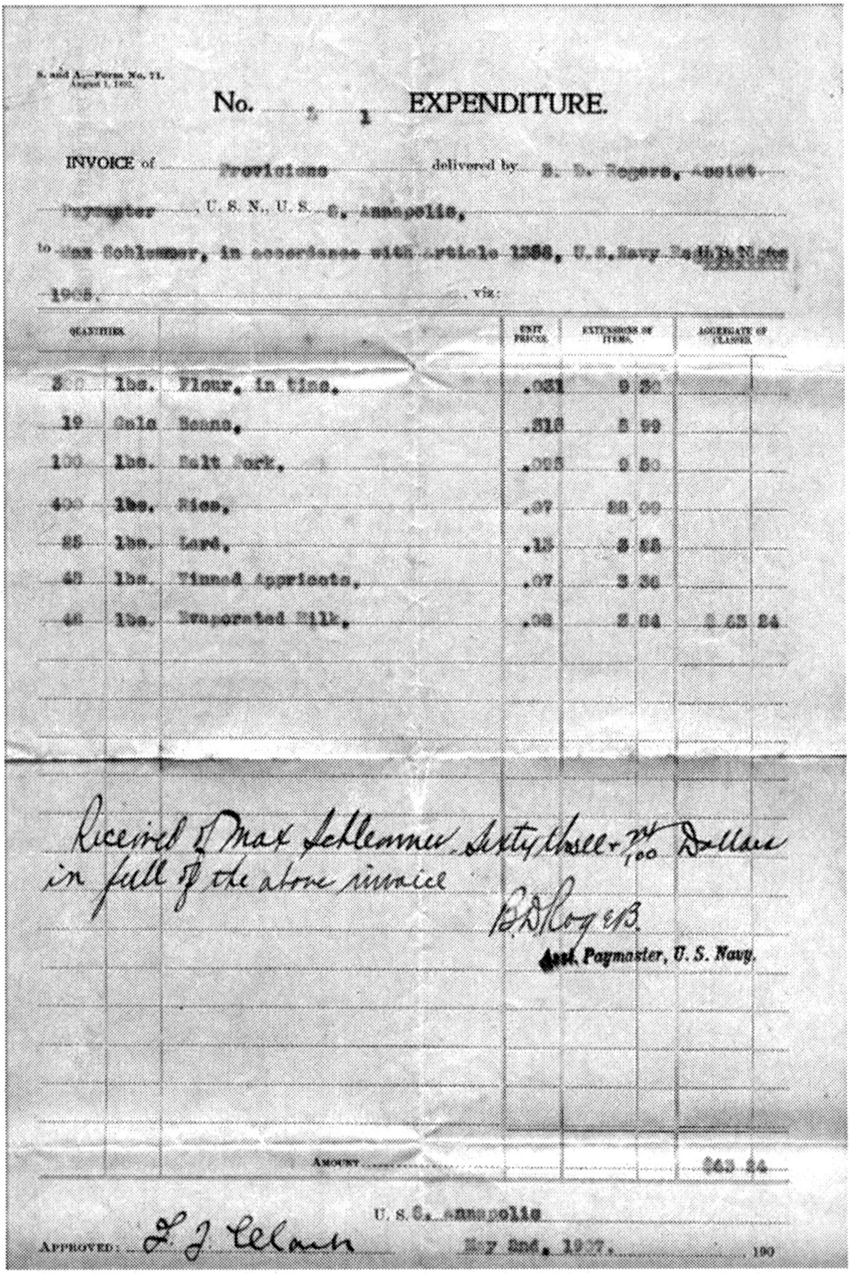

S. and A.—Form No. 11.
August 1, 190[illegible]

No. [illegible] 1 EXPENDITURE.

INVOICE of Provisions delivered by B. D. Rogers, Assist. Paymaster, U. S. N., U. S. S. Annapolis,

to Max Schlemmer, in accordance with Article 1288, U.S.Navy Reg[illegible]

1905, viz:

QUANTITIES.			UNIT PRICES.	EXTENSIONS OF ITEMS.	AGGREGATE OF CLASSES.
3[illegible]	lbs.	Flour, in tins,	.031	9 30	
19	Gals	Beans,	.316	5 99	
100	lbs.	Salt Pork,	.095	9 50	
400	lbs.	Rice,	.07	28 00	
25	lbs.	Lard,	.13	3 25	
48	lbs.	Tinned Appricots,	.07	3 36	
48	lbs.	Evaporated Milk,	.08	3 84	$ 63 24

Received of Max Schlemmer Sixty three + 24/100 Dollars in full of the above invoice

B.D. Rogers
Asst. Paymaster, U. S. Navy.

AMOUNT $63 24

U. S. S. Annapolis

APPROVED: L. J. Clark May 2nd, 1907. 190

A provision receipt in the year 1907

COAST GUARD CUTTER
THETIS

TREASURY DEPARTMENT

UNITED STATES COAST GUARD

Honolulu, T.H. December 23, 1915.

Mr. Max Schlemmer,

    1160 Gulick Avenue,

        Honolulu, T.H.

                Subject: Information desired; poachers
                        last winter.

My dear Sir:

    1. I have your communication of the other day
and in reply thereto wish to state that in my opinion there
is nothing to be done until word from Washington has been
received.

    2. Kindly keep me informed of anything that you
might learn as to which party or parties were poaching on Laysan
Island last winter.

    3. With best wishes, I am,

                Sincerely yours,

                1st. Lieut. U.S.C.G.

Answer to Max's complaint regarding bird poaching at Laysan Island

C. Q. YEE HOP & CO., Ltd.

WHOLESALE AND RETAIL BUTCHERS

NO. 125 KING STREET, NEAR FISH MARKET

HONOLULU, T. H., _____ 191___

BILLS PAYABLE MONTHLY. INTEREST CHARGED AFTER MATURITY

IMPORTERS AND COMMISSION MERCHANTS

POST OFFICE BOX 1013
PHONE 3451 PHONE

Order for supplies

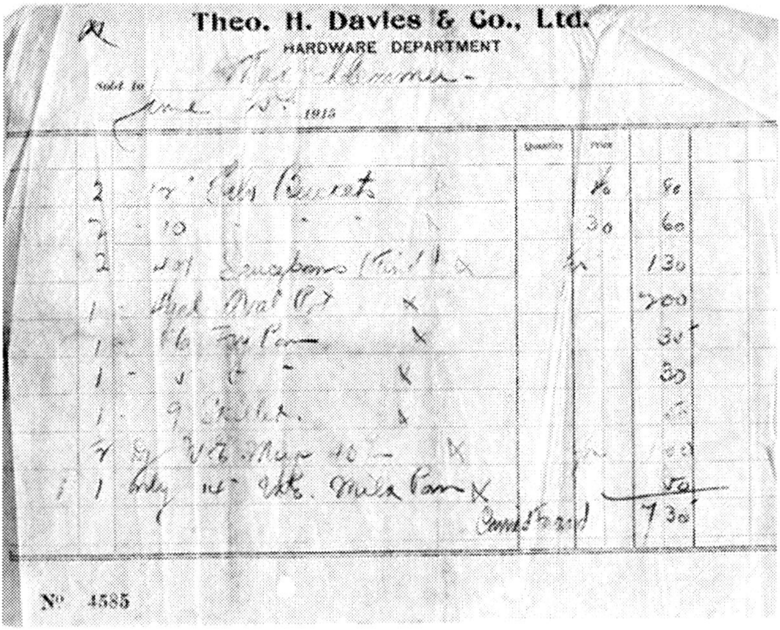

Theo. H. Davies & Co., Ltd.
HARDWARE DEPARTMENT
Sold to Max Schlemmer
June 1915
No. 4585

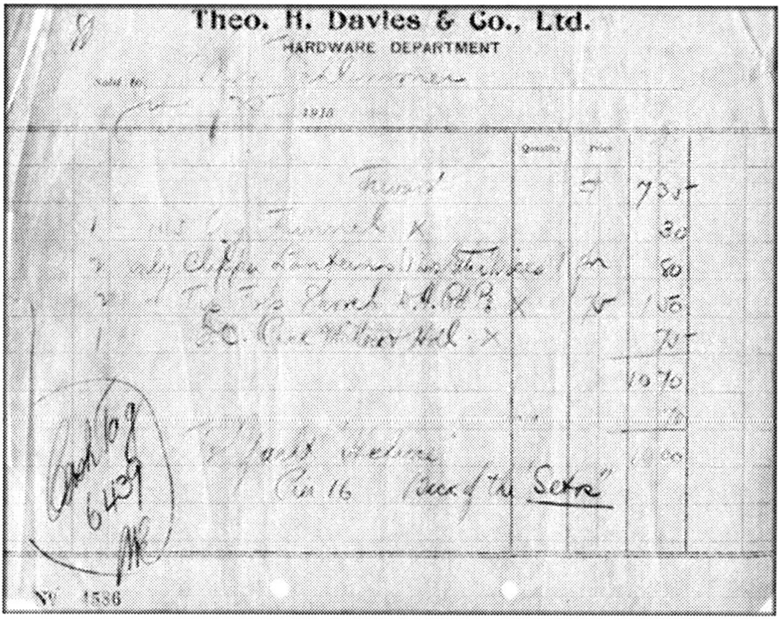

Theo. H. Davies & Co., Ltd.
HARDWARE DEPARTMENT
Sold to
1915
No. 4586

Receipts for supplies

TREASURY DEPARTMENT,
U. S. PUBLIC HEALTH SERVICE,
Form 1984.
Ed. 50,000—P. C., Jan. 30-14.

PORT SANITARY STATEMENT,

U. S. PUBLIC HEALTH SERVICE.

Port of _____ Honolulu, T.H. _____

Vessel: _____ YACHT HELENE _____

Bound from _____ Honolulu _____ *to* _____ South Sea Islands _____

Number of cases of and deaths from the following-named diseases reported during the two weeks ending _____ July 4, _____ 191 4.

DISEASES.	NUMBER OF CASES.	NUMBER OF DEATHS.	REMARKS. (Any condition affecting the public health existing in the port to be stated here, including operations to rodent examination and examination.)
Cerebro-spinal Meningitis (epidemic)	----	----	Last case rat plague Kukuihaele,
Cholera, Asiatic	----	----	Hawaii January 30, 1914.
Diphtheria	4	1	Last case human plague Honokaa
Measles	----	----	Hawaii, June 11, 1914.
Plague	----	----	Trapping and examination of
Poliomyelitis (inflam. acute)	----	----	rodents regularly carried
Scarlet Fever	----	----	out at this port.
Smallpox	----	----	
Typhoid Fever	----	----	
Typhus Fever	----	----	
Yellow Fever	----	----	
TOTALS	4	1	

Vessel last fumigated at _____ , 19 __

Given under my hand and seal this _____ 16th _____ *day of* _____ July _____ , 191 4.

[SEAL]

F. E. Trotter

Sur. H. S.   Surgeon, U. S. Public Health Service.

Sanitary Inspection Certificate for the *Helene* allowing her to leave Pearl
Harbor on her last trip to Laysan Island

CEIVED FROM ATKINS, KROLL & CO., the sum of five hundred and twenty-five dollars ($525.00) in full satisfaction of any and all claims that the undersigned, Max Schlemmer, may have against the said Atkins, Kroll & Co., or against any of the owners, or against the master or crew of the wrecked schooner "O.M.Kellogg" for any services of any nature whatsoever rendered to date, and in particular all services in connection with transporting the master, the master's wife, and the crew of the said schooner from Laysan Island to Midway Island; and in full satisfaction of any and all claims that the said Max Schlemmer, or any other owner of the sloop "Helene", may have against the parties aforesaid by reason of the loan of the sloop "Helene" made to the master of said schooner in October, 1915, to carry them from Laysan Island to Midway Island, and by reason of the subsequent accident to said sloop and of any and all damages which the undersigned may have suffered by the loss of said sloop.

San Francisco, California,
June 2nd, 1916.

Max Schlemmer

By Mc Clanahan & Derby.

His attorneys, authorized to
make this settlement on behalf of said Max Schlemmer.

A settlement letter for the loss of the *Helene*

ATKINS, KROLL & CO.

CABLES: "ATISCO"
CODES: A B C, 6TH AND 5TH EDITIONS
    WESTERN UNION
    LIEBER'S
    A. I.

TELEPHONE: KEARNY 2543 (2 LINES)

311 CALIFORNIA ST.

SAN FRANCISCO. Dec. 22, 1915.

Max Schlemmer, Esq.
    1160 Gulick Ave.,
        Honolulu, T.H.

Dear Sir:

We are in receipt of your favor of Dec.14th, and
contents have our attention.

Captain Lunn, of our schooner "O.M.Kellogg",
has reported to us your kind action in loaning him your Sloop
Yacht "Helene" and we very much appreciate this and thank
you for having rendered this assistance.

We understand from Captain Lunn, that you are
desirous of having the Government return your yacht to
Laysan Island, and we have already taken this matter
up with the Government at Washington. As soon as we have
any definite reply, regarding this matter, we shall advise
you. In the meantime, we note that you do not mention
having the yacht returned to Laysan in your letter and we are
wondering if it will now suit you better to have the yacht stay
at Midway Island. We shall be glad to hear definitely from
you on this point.

With regard to the accusation which had been made
against you, accusing you of being a German spy, we note
your remarks. We are sending a copy of your letter on to
Washington and this will be given to the proper authorities
there.

Awaiting the favor of your reply, and again
thanking you for your kindness to our ship-wrecked crew, we
beg to remain,

Yours very truly,

ATKINS, KROLL & CO

CHK.

Letter to Max prior to loss of the *Helene*

SLOOP HELENE LOST AT MIDWAY ISLAND: WIND IS HURRICANE

News of still another wreck was received in Honolulu yesterday. This time it is the sloop Helene, owned by Max Schlemmer. The captain received a cablegram from Midway Island yesterday that she went ashore Friday during a heavy westerly gale.

Breaking from her moorings, the Helene ran on the shoals, about one hundred yards from the cable pier, and broke up Saturday afternoon, some of the wreckage being washed up on the beach. The gale, then north northwest, continued Sunday, blowing at times with hurricane force, with occasional hail showers. This was the second time in thirteen years that hail has fallen at Midway, where the station of the Commercial Pacific Cable Company is located.

The sloop and Max Schlemmer have had adventures a-plenty since June, when the captain sailed for Laysan Island. The schooner O. M. Kellogg was wrecked on Maro reef in September, and the crew made Laysan in the ship's boat. At Laysan the men borrowed the sloop from Schlemmer to go to Midway, whence they were brought to the United States Navy tug Iroquois, which made a special voyage for them. Schlemmer and his two companions were taken from Laysan by the United States Navy collier Nereus in November.

New mooring buoys were planted by the Iroquois when she was at Midway for mooring the Helene.

This report of bad weather at Midway proves that the Pacific is not at all pacific these days. Gales near the coast, at the Islands, south of Fiji and at Midway show general bad weather.

Newspaper clipping about loss of Helene

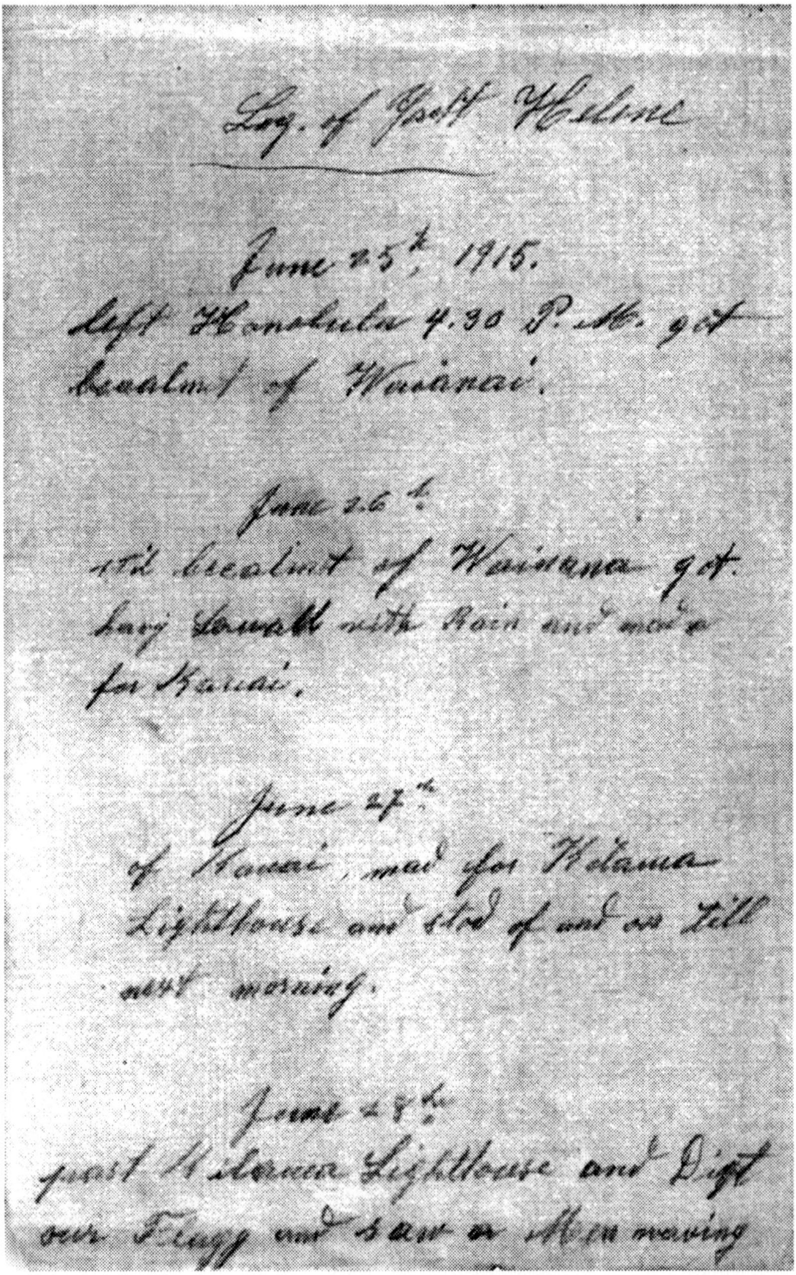

Log. of Yacht Helene

June 25th, 1915.
Left Honolulu 4.30 P.M. got
becalmt of Waianai.

June 26th
still becalmt of Waianae got
lazy squall with Rain and made
for Kauai.

June 27th
of Kauai, mad for Kilauea
Lighthouse and stod of and on till
next morning.

June 28th
past Kilauea Lighthouse and Dipt
our Flagg and saw a Man waving

Page 1 of the log of the *Helene*

his Boat past Hawaii and dipt
our Flagg to Mr: Birkmeyer and
other Friends of old. I am past
Waimea and dipt our Flagg to
Mrs George Titcomb and other old
Hawaiians, and was next around toars
Kona mae me were becalmd

June 29th
still becalm est of Kona Point
we met a Sampan with 3 japanese
I askt them were the were going and the
said Fish husnahuwa there were
lots N.N.W.

June 30th
got light Wind and made for Waimea
not able to get in before dark I hauld

GENERAL OFFICE

AMERICAN FACTORS, LIMITED

CAPITAL $ 6,000,000

SUGAR FACTORS

WHOLESALE & COMMISSION MERCHANTS

INSURANCE

SAN FRANCISCO
NEW YORK

TELEGRAPHIC ADDRESS
"AMFACTORS"
WESTERN UNION

HONOLULU, HAWAII   Sept. 1, 1927.

Capt. Max Schlemmer,

Honolulu.

My dear Captain:

As the years roll by, for all of us a time
will come when each and everyone of us must turn over
his duties to younger men.   This Company has been very
fortunate in having you with it for the great number
of years that you have been connected with the firm,
and the services that you have rendered have been as
conscientious and faithful as any man could render;
but nevertheless owing to the passing of the years the
time has now come when you for your own good should
turn over the reins which you have held for so long to
a younger man in order that you may in the years to
come take life easier than you have done in the past.

In recognition of the faithful services which
you have rendered this Company, which are deeply appreciated by everyone who has been associated with you, it
gives us pleasure to advise you that until further notice the Company will pay to you each month the sum of
$100.00.

Trusting we may have the pleasure of seeing
you from time to time, we remain

Yours very truly,

AMERICAN FACTORS, LIMITED.

S. M. Lowrey,
Treasurer.

Max's Retirement letter

JAMES D. LEVENSON
HONOLULU

HONOLULU, HAWAII, February 7, 1916.

As you are aware, our fellow townsman, Mr. Max Schlemmer, has recently been returned from Laysan Island, which is one of the group of small islands forming the Hawaiian Island Bird Reservation and therefore under the jurisdiction of the U. S. Biological Survey. Owing to the timely and generous assistance rendered by Mr. Schlemmer to the ten members of the shipwrecked crew of the O. M. Kellogg last September and the use of his vessel by them which was left by these unfortunate people at Midway, he is back in Honolulu without his vessel and without employment.

There should be a warden stationed on Laysan to guard at all seasons the wonderful bird colonies there from further depredations and to assist shipwrecked and distressed vessels in the windward chain of islands. There is reason to hope that the Biological Survey will soon supplement the work of the Thetis and appoint a regular resident warden for this great bird reservation. It is to be hoped that Mr. Schlemmer will receive this position since it is one he is well fitted to fill.

But in the meantime Mr. Schlemmer and his family are in need of temporary help. I therefore bring this matter to your attention, trusting that you will respond and assist this man who has lived long in these islands and in this instance, as well as in others that need not be mentioned, has rendered assistance of such a nature that the community should not be willing to see him suffer as a result of his humane acts on Laysan.

Please make your check payable to Max Schlemmer, and mail same in the enclosed envelope. Mr. Schlemmer will send acknowledgments personally.

Very truly yours,

P.S.—Above all Mr. Schlemmer wants employment and will be obliged if you can furnish him work or tell him where he can find a temporary or permanent job.

Letter to the community asking them to help the Schlemmer Family

Hon. Delegate Prince Jonah Kalanianaole,

    Dear Sir:-

        I herewith would kindly ask you to help me secure the position as warden for the north west group of Bird reserve Islands, as I have been recommended for the same by Rear-Admiral Chauncey, Commander in chief of the U. S. Pacific Fleet; Prof. Wm. A. Bryant; and Captain A. P. Niblack of the U. S. Navy; and as I have been a resident here for forty-one (41) years and have a family of twelve (12) children to support and have always done what's right but did not believe of being robbed of my rights as an American citizen, I will therefore inclose you a copy of "Happenings on the Islands of Laysan and Lisianski" as near as I can remember.

        Trusting in you

        I remain

        Yours Respectfully

        Max Schlemmer

Letter from Max requesting help in getting the Federal Warden's Position for the islands of Laysan and Lisianski

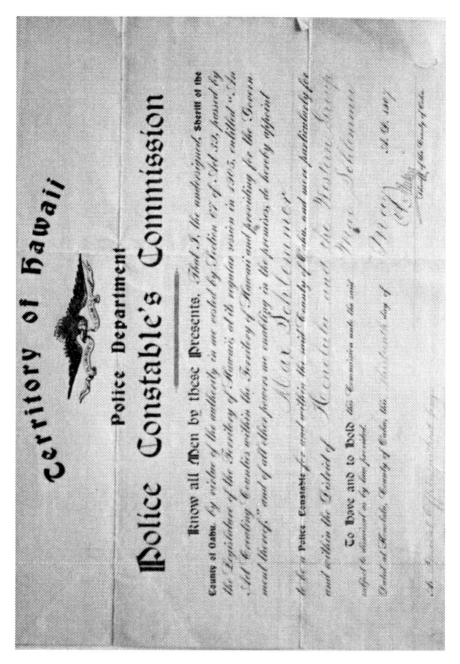

Certificate for Police Constable's Commission, Territory of Hawaii

BIBLIOGRAPHY

Bailey, Alfred M. *Laysan and the Black Footed Albatross*, Museum Pictorial, Denver Museum of Natural History, July 15, 1952.

Bailey, Alfred M. *The Hawaiian Monk Seal*, Museum Pictorial, Denver Museum of Natural History, August 1, 1952.

Bailey, Alfred M. *Birds of Midway and Laysan Islands,* Museum Pictorial, Denver Museum of Natural History, September 4, 1956.

Bensen, Bruce. "Laysan Island, The Last Refuge," *The Honolulu Advertiser*, April 8, 1973.

Bryan, Dr. E.H. *Laysan, an Island of the Pacific, Paradise of the Pacific*, May 1938.

Bryan, William A. *Laysan Island, A Visit to Hawaii's Bird Reservation, Mid Pacific Magazine*, October 1911.

Carus, Jr. Edward H. *Forgotten Islands of the Hawaiian Archapellago,* Ka-`Elele. Bishop Museum, December 1990.

Day, A. Grove. *History Makers of Hawaii,* Mutual Publishing, 1984.

Day, A. Grove. *Mad About Islands*, Mutual Publishing. 1987.

Day, A. Grove. *Mark Twain's Letters From Hawaii,* University of Hawaii Press, 1975.

Ely, Charles A. and Clapp. *Natural History of Laysan Island,* Smithsonian Institution 1973.

Gast, Ross H. *Traveling Hawaiian Byways With Pen and Camera,* Old Blanc House Press, 1936.

Krauss, Bob and Alexander, *W.P. Grove Farm Plantation,* Pacific Books, 1976.

Lipman, Victor. "Life, Death and Rebirth of an Island," Honolulu Magazine, November 1984.

MacIntyre, Ian G. *Atoll Research Bulletin,* Smithsonian Institution, 1996.

Mellen, George. *Sales Builder, Pacific Guano and Fertilizer Co. Ltd.,* Star Bulletin Printing House, 1939.

Mifflin, Thomas. *Schooner From Windward,* University of Hawaii Press, 1983.

Morris, Penrose G. *How The Territory of Hawaii Grew and What Domain It Covered,* Hawaii Historial Report, 1933.

Rayson, Ann. *Modern Hawaiian,* Bess Press, 1984.

Swchweizer, *Niklua R. Hawaii and the German Speaking People,* Top Gallant Publishing, 1982.

Whitten, Harry. *Laysan-born Islander Recalls Mining Days, The Honolulu Star Bulletin*, March 13, 1980.

Wisniewski, Richard. "Hawaii, the Territorial Years," Pacific Basin Enterprises, 1984.

Yamashita, Stanley. "Forgotten Hawaii, the Leeward Islands," *The Sunday Star Bulletin and Advertiser,* Honolulu, October 13, 1968.

ABOUT THE AUTHOR

Tom Unger was born in Honolulu, June 12, 1923. He is a graduate of Roosevelt High School, 1941, and the University of Portland, 1950.

He received a combat commission and Purple Heart while serving with the 88th Infantry Division during World War II in Italy.

Tom was manager of General Mills Inc. in Hawaii and later held the same position with Beatrice Foods in Hawaii, on Okinawa and in Korea. He returned to Hawaii in 1972 and was a pioneer in the marketing of macadamia nuts. In 1977, he was president of the Hawaii Macadamia Nut Growers Association.

Tom and his wife Janice, were proprietors of the Honomu Plantation Store on the island of Hawaii for nine years until their retirement in 1988. They have six children and ten grandchildren. Tom and Janice presently reside in Honolulu.

0-595-29988-1